From At Risk to Academic Excellence

What Successful Leaders Do

Franklin P. Schargel
Tony Thacker
John S. Bell

EYE ON EDUCATION
6 DEPOT WAY WEST, SUITE 106
LARCHMONT, NY 10538
(914) 833–0551
(914) 833–0761 fax
www.eyeoneducation.com

Library of Congress Cataloging-in-Publication Data

Schargel, Franklin P.
From at-risk to academic excellence : What Successful Leaders Do / Franklin
P. Schargel, Tony Thacker, John S. Bell.
        p. cm.
    ISBN 1-59667-046-0
1. Educational leadership—United States. 2. School improvement pro-
grams—United States. 3. Academic achievement—United States. I. Thacker,
Tony, 1959- II. Bell, John S., 1949- III. Title.
LB2805.S318 2007
371.2—dc22

                                                            2007002429

10 9 8 7 6 5 4 3 2

Editorial and production services provided by
Richard H. Adin Freelance Editorial Services
52 Oakwood Blvd., Poughkeepsie, NY 12603-4112
(845-471-3566)

Also Available from EYE ON EDUCATION

Best Practices to Help At-Risk Learners
Franklin P. Schargel

Helping Students Graduate
Jay Smink and Franklin P. Schargel

Dropout Prevention Tools
Franklin P. Schargel

Strategies to Help Solve Our School Dropout Problem
Franklin P. Schargel and Jay Smink

Classroom Motivation from A to Z:
How to Engage Your Students in Learning
Barbara R. Blackburn

Classroom Instruction from A to Z:
How to Promote Student Learning
Barbara R. Blackburn

Teach Me – I Dare You
Judith Brough, Sherrel Bergmann, and Larry Holt

How to Reach and Teach All Students: Simplified!
Elizabeth Breaux

101 "Answers" for New Teachers and Their Mentors:
Effective Teaching Tips for Daily Classroom Use
Annette L. Breaux

Handbook on Differentiated Instruction
for Middle and High Schools
Sheryn Spencer Northey

At-Risk Students:
Reaching and Teaching Them, Second Edition
Richard Sagor and Jonas Cox

The Handbook for Developing
Supportive Learning Environments
Teddy Holtz Frank

What Great Principals Do *Differently*:
15 Things That Matter Most
Todd Whitaker

What Successful Principals Do!
169 Tips for Principals
Franzy Fleck

Improving Your School One Week At a Time:
Building the Foundation for Professional Teaching & Learning
Jeffrey Zoul

Lead With Me:
A Principal's Guide to Teacher Leadership
Gayle Moller and Anita Pankake

The Instructional Leader's Guide
to Informal Classroom Observations
Sally J. Zepeda

Lead Me – I Dare You!
Sherrel Bergman and Judith Brough

Countdown to the Principalship:
A Resource Guide for Beginning Principals
O'Rourke, Provenzano, Bellamy, and Ballek

Smart, Fast, Efficient:
The New Principals' Guide to Success
Leanna Stohr Isaacson

BRAVO Principal!
Sandra Harris

The Administrator's Guide
to School Community Relations, Second Edition
George E. Pawlas

School Leader Internship: Developing, Monitoring, and Evaluating
Your Leadership Experience, Second Edition
Martin, Wright, Danzig, Flanary, and Brown

The Principal as Instructional Leader:
A Handbook for Supervisors
Sally J. Zepeda

Acknowledgments

As this book clearly states in its title and text, we are concerned with education leadership of our at-risk learners. We must start by applauding the hardworking teachers and school administrators who daily face the challenge of educating our most needy youth. Many young people face obstacles in their personal lives and homes that most of our readers cannot imagine. These educators frequently do more good than the media, politicians, and many business leaders wish to acknowledge. We dedicate this book to those dedicated, overworked, and underpaid individuals who give so much of their time and energy so that others might thrive in the 21st century.

Like you, the reader, I have been greatly influenced by some of my teachers. I would like to thank all of those who have helped me achieve whatever success I have had. I would like to start with my parents, Aaron and Pauline Schargel, who taught me to keep fighting for what I believed was right. Thanks also to my wife, Sandy, who never had doubts about my work and has always been there in front leading me, alongside me as a friend, and behind me making sure I persevered; and to my children, David, Pegi, and Howard, who have taught me more than I could I ever teach them.

We also acknowledge the friends and colleagues who helped form the direction of the book and made suggestions as we wrote, especially Lynn Ritvo; Ed Bales, formerly of Motorola; Lewis A. Rappaport, my friend and former principal, for recognizing my abilities and for giving me a chance to prove my worth; Ella Bell of the Alabama State Board of Education; Dr. Myron Tribus; and Mike DeWitte of Sandia National Labs. We thank Dr. Jay Smink and the associates of the National Dropout Prevention Center who helped us formulate the book and provide the education community and the nation an invaluable resource for our at-risk children. I am grateful to my publisher, Robert Sickles, who has been there from the beginning and provided the inspiration for this book, and to Celia Bohannon, who transformed our string of words into a strand of pearls. And to my co-authors, Tony and John, I cannot tell you how wonderful it was to work with you.

Finally, thanks to my teachers at PS 191, JHS 210, and Thomas Jefferson High School, who put up with a highly quizzical individual. You might want to know that your efforts were not wasted.

Franklin Schargel

I would first like to acknowledge my parents, Jim and Sandy Thacker, for providing me with the guidance I so surely needed as I was growing up. I will always appreciate that you saw more in me than I often did myself. I would also like to thank my dear wife, Annette, for staying beside me through good times and bad and for being the kindest soul that I have ever met. Your love has filled my life with great joy. Nothing I ever accomplish professionally or personally will compare to the importance I place on honoring you as my wife and best friend.

I would like to thank my two coauthors, Franklin and John, for their friendship, camaraderie, and laughter. Whatever I gain from this book can never equal the value of the knowledge I have gained from the two of you. To Dr. Morton, Dr. Ash, and Dr. Commander, thank you for providing the type of environment at the Alabama Department of Education that engenders continuous learning and a yearning to do better. The children of Alabama will benefit from your leadership. To Dr. Ron Lindahl, my mentor and friend, thank you for being an exemplar of all that is right with education. Your many kindnesses have brightened my life immensely.

Finally, I would like to acknowledge the finest man I ever had the pleasure of knowing and who, tragically, passed away far too soon. Mike Schovel was the closest thing to a Renaissance man I ever met. His curiosity and thirst for knowledge drove him to learn as much as he could about everything he touched. Although he was demanding of our students, all of whom were at risk, he was profoundly human with each and every one. He gave of himself to every man, woman, and child he ever met; and he left a legacy of kindness and humility that those who knew him will never forget. The world was a far happier place with Mike in it, but our loss is heaven's gain. Still, I miss you, Mike, and so do many, many others.

Tony Thacker

Special thanks to Governor Bob Riley; Dr. Joseph Morton, state superintendent of education; and Dr. Ruth Ash, deputy state superintendent of education, for continued support of leadership development in Alabama. Their guidance and vision have made school leadership in Alabama a key issue. This book is a testament to their conscientiousness, conversation, and collaboration around the issues of improving school leadership for the children of Alabama. I also want to thank the many educators in my life who, over the years, taught me that there is no more noble profession and no more worthy goal than to help others reach their full potential.

I want to thank my son, Andy, for being my best and most loyal student. Having been both his middle and high school principal, I am not sure who learned more. Your children keep you safe and give you the most important reason for being a lifelong learner. Most of all, I want to thank my wife, Lorna, who shows me every day that life is what one makes it and that against the toughest odds, with positive thinking and much effort, one can achieve anything. She has been and remains my greatest teacher.

John Bell

Meet the Authors

Franklin Schargel, a native of Brooklyn now residing in Albuquerque, New Mexico, is a graduate of the University of the City of New York. Franklin holds a master's degree in secondary education from City University and another in school administration and supervision from Pace University. His career spans 33 years of classroom teaching and counseling and 8 years of supervision and administration as assistant principal. In addition, Franklin taught a course in Dowling College's MBA program.

Franklin served on the Guidelines Development Committee for the Malcolm Baldrige National Quality Award in Education and was for 2 years an examiner for the Baldrige Award. In addition, he served as a judge for the Secretary of the Air Force Quality Award and a judge for the USA Today/RIT Quality Cup. He recently completed his term as chair of the American Society of Quality's Education Division.

As senior managing associate of his training firm, School Success Network, Franklin has presented countless workshops for educational, community, and business groups throughout the United States, Europe, Canada, and Latin America. His workshops are for administrators, teachers, students, parents, business leaders, policymakers, and anyone else interested in building world-class schools. They cover a wide variety of topics, including dealing with at-risk school populations, dropout prevention, consensus building, curriculum innovation, educational leadership, empowerment of staff, interactive learning, the Malcolm Baldrige National Quality Award in Education, organizational change, parental involvement, problem solving, Career and Technical Education, strategic planning, student evaluation and data analysis, teamwork, tech prep, and Total Quality Education. All his workshops are tailored to the individual client's needs and expected outcomes.

He is the author of five well-received books: *Transforming Education Through Total Quality Management: A Practitioner's Guide; Strategies to Help Solve Our School Dropout Problem; Dropout Prevention Tools; Helping Students Graduate;* and *Best Practices to Help At-Risk Learners,* as well as more than 65 articles published in leading educational journals and business magazines. Mr. Schargel has a regular monthly Internet column at www.guidance channel. com/.

Franklin's success in dramatically enhancing the learning process in his inner-city school, expanding parental involvement, increasing postsecondary school attendance, and significantly lowering the students' dropout rate has been well documented in 25 books, 55 newspaper and magazine articles (including *Business Week, Fortune,* and the *New York Times*), and five internationally released videos (including a Public Broadcasting special).

In 2005, Mr. Schargel received the Crystal Star Award from the National Dropout Prevention Center for "substantially reducing the number of dropouts in the country."

Dr. Tony Thacker is a member of the Classroom Improvement section of the Alabama Department of Education. His current role is the project administrator for the Governor's Commission on Quality Teaching. He has served as a principal, science teacher, and national trainer for the University of Alabama's integrated science program and he initiated the Torchbearer School Program. Dr. Thacker speaks to groups across the nation regarding leadership in education, leading change, and the need for true reform on all levels.

Although he is proud to be an educator, he is quick to add that his proudest accomplishment is his 20-year marriage to his wife, Annette.

John Bell is coordinator of leadership development at the Alabama Department of Education. In his 31 years as an educator, John was a high school teacher, a middle school principal, a high school principal, a headmaster, and a university adjunct instructor. He spent 18 years in Alabama's Montgomery Public School System. John was selected Teacher of the Year and named Administrator of the Year by the Alabama Art Educators Association.

A group leader at the Harvard University Graduate School of Education's Principals' Center, John has also served as a member of the Harvard Principals' Center Advisory Board.

Besides coordinating the Alabama Leadership Academy, John is also the project administrator for Governor Bob Riley's Congress on School Leadership. The Governor's Congress on School Leadership is a comprehensive initiative to support improved school leadership in Alabama by recommending changes in standards, selection and university preparation, professional development, certification, and removal of on-the-job barriers.

Foreword

Accountability and higher standards have changed just about every aspect of education. Legislation has established an exigency to improve student achievement in an educational system that supports a culture of status quo and results in the failure of far too many students. This era of higher standards, greater accountability, and more at-risk students requires a new kind of school and district leader who can inspire teachers, parents, and the community to coalesce and provide better opportunities for all students to achieve at high levels.

We must improve the way we prepare school leaders and ensure that they have an instructional focus rather than one of management. We must improve the professional growth we give our teachers and leaders and ensure that it is aligned with standards and the needs for school improvement. And finally, we must organize and run schools for the benefit of the students, not the comforts of educators.

From At Risk to Academic Excellence: What Successful Leaders Do provides examples of places where schools should be failing but, in reality, they are helping students to achieve at high levels. These schools have dedicated teachers led by an instructional leader who has student achievement as the main goal of the school. These examples are also beacons of hope for educators who are sometimes frustrated by the quality of education we see in many of our schools. It says we can do it and here is the proof.

Use this book as a reminder of what we already know and of what can be accomplished. Authors Franklin Schargel, Tony Thacker, and John Bell have provided much food for thought. They show us examples of places where students are learning, faculty are energized, and leaders keep instruction and learning in the forefront.

The time to act is now. Never before has the need been more urgent for a well educated work force. Never before have the problems associated with at-risk students been more apparent. And never before has change been an absolute. This book highlights the abundance of data available about the plight of at-risk students and reminds us that we know what to do to help students achieve at high levels, but often fail to do it. It challenges all of us to implement what will benefit students even if it disturbs the comfort of educators.

Dr. Gene Bottoms, Vice President
Southern Regional Education Board

Table of Contents

Part I

Setting a New Focus

1

A New Reality

The reality is that the majority of American schools are places where the pieces simply do not fit together and there is very little that the teachers in those schools can do about it.

Marc Tucker

Events of the past 50 years have dramatically altered the world's economic, social, and political landscape. Our former military enemies have joined us in pursuit of peace and prosperity. The harsh dictatorships of the Soviet Union, Eastern Europe, and Iraq have either fallen or been toppled. Europe has drawn together into a new entity, the European Union. Industrialized nations have seen their populations grow older as birth rates decline. The world has merged into one competitive marketplace. Its burgeoning middle class is clamoring for increased services in health, transportation, and education. China and India, once regarded as sleeping tigers, have expanded and strengthened their educational systems and are fast catching up with other industrialized nations. Schools around the world face pressure to produce globally competitive, first-rate graduates.

America has reached a pinnacle of world power and influence. Our abundant natural resources, robust economy, and strong democratic system contributed to this rise; but the bedrock of our nation's prosperity and freedom is the public education program initiated more than 200 years ago. If we wish to sustain these remarkable achievements, we must improve the existing school system to accommodate a new reality.

At its best, education develops responsible citizens; inspires a love of learning; cultivates an appreciation of art, music, and literature; promotes cultural and social values; and builds the nation's workforce. Our educational system continues to prepare our future doctors, teachers, political and economic leaders, entrepreneurs, and artists. Even the sports figures our youth admire learn their values in school. Tomorrow's good jobs will require advanced training and schooling that build on the indispensable foundation of a high school diploma. Tomorrow's workforce needs the ability to problem solve, work on teams, keep up with fast-changing technology, and efficiently use resources. Underachievement in school limits the future prosperity of today's students and their families. It also holds the United States back in the global marketplace.

The Social Security Administration estimates that Americans older than 65 years of age will constitute 20% of the total population by 2030—up from 13% in 1998. This means more retirees drawing benefits and fewer workers paying taxes. When the 76 million baby boomers leave the workforce, today's cohort of students will have to take up the slack. To maintain our nation's productivity in this information and knowledge age, we must equip them with the skills and competencies to do their jobs. An educated workforce will earn more, increasing the tax base, and carry more responsibility, improving our society and economy. But to achieve all this, we must keep today's young people in school.

Who Will Teach Our Kids?

Educators, politicians, and businesspeople all agree that leadership in education has never been more critical for public school systems. They also share a grave concern about the looming shortage of qualified educational leaders.

On October 2, 2000, the headline on the cover of *Newsweek* cover read, "Who Will Teach Our Kids?" The accompanying story projected that over the next 10 years, 2.2 million teachers—of the existing workforce of 2.6 million—would leave the profession because of retirement, low pay, low morale, frustration with the educational system, and better opportunities elsewhere.

Yet, the crisis is not just limited to teachers. According to *USA Today*, "Roughly half of the nation's superintendents are older than age 50 and will likely leave their jobs in the next five years....Those officials worry that there are not enough qualified candidates to fill the vacancies" (Henry, 2000). The article went on to quote Mary Lee Fitzgerald, director of education programs for the Wallace Reader's Digest Fund, Inc., "The principalship is a bull market. Nobody wants the job. Modest pay, long hours, uneven resources, problematic authority, increased expectations of the public make this job in a competitive market a no-winner for the top half of the class."

The job of school superintendent is often the least stable position in the school district. Tenure averages just 36 months (less in our inner-city school districts). According to the Council of the Great City Schools (2003), "The average tenure of the current Great City School superintendent increased from 2½ years in 2001 to 2¾ years in 2003. The majority of superintendents (54 percent) have been in office one to five years. Approximately 31 percent...have been in office for one year or less. Only 15 percent...had five or more years in their current position." However, a superintendent must learn the culture of the district, develop a strategic plan for school improvement, and then deploy that plan—a difficult, if not impossible, task to accomplish in 3 years or less.

A New Population of Students

According to the U.S. Department of Education (Troy, 1998), our nation has 87,125 schools in 14,471 districts and 46.3 million students in public school classrooms. More than 6.2 million children have limited English proficiency; 2 million speak no English. Two million latchkey children go home to an empty house; another two million endure abuse and neglect at home. An estimated 1 million children suffer from the effects of lead poisoning, a major cause of slow learning; more than 500,000 come from foster and institutional care; 30,000 are products of fetal alcohol syndrome. Nearly 400,000 are *crack babies* and children of other drug users. More than half a million are homeless, lacking a permanent address. Of children younger than 18, approximately 20% (14.4 million) come from homes with extreme poverty. More than half of poor children are white and live in rural and suburban areas. And America's schools are taking in growing minority populations from countries that lack strong educational infrastructures.

Principals and superintendents must respond to a host of new challenges: diversity of cultural backgrounds, waves of immigration, income disparities, physical and mental disabilities, and variation in learning capability. Increasingly, schools must adapt to address the needs of at-risk, nontraditional learners. Wherever teacher education programs have not kept pace with these challenges, many of their graduates must learn on the job, under the tutelage of their school leaders. And the tasks of scheduling, programming, ensuring security, and providing counseling have all become more complex.

When Henry Ford's company sold its first cars, he famously stated, "You can have any color you want as long as it's black." Ford's plants were set up accordingly. Ford Motor Company could not address the needs of today's public if it were still only offering one choice. Schools can no longer afford to offer *one-size-fits-all* education; today's society demands an individualized approach that caters to the needs of each child. Today's educational leaders cannot rely solely on traditional methods of teaching and learning; they need a new repertoire of skills and approaches.

New Responsibilities Require New Qualifications

In the olden days, we could sum up the principal's role in a few words: to manage the building and head the school; to be a *pal* to students, parents and teachers; to be a leader of teachers. But that role has dramatically expanded. Consider the leadership responsibilities outlined for today's principals:

Leadership Responsibilities

Principal as a Leader

- Facilitate and implement a comprehensively developed and shared vision and mission.
  - Implementation must include the development of structures to support the vision and mission.
- Create a culture of high expectations for all students.

- Expectations must be communicated to staff, students, parents, and the wider community; and actions must consistently reflect those expectations.
  - Model ethical conduct and universally expect the same from faculty and staff.
    - Expectations must be clearly explained and consistently enforced.
  - Empower others to make significant decisions.
    - Expanding the foundation of leadership stabilizes any organization.
  - Nurture teacher involvement and engender teacher leadership.
    - Teacher leaders take ownership of the school and its processes.
    - Comprehensive input and involvement in the decision-making processes improves the chances of making the best available decision.

Principal as a Lead Teacher and Learner

- Sustain a school culture conducive to student and staff learning.
  - Ensure the use of research-based strategies that support a cooperatively developed curriculum.
  - Promote the use of research-based programs as a means of achieving the school's objectives.
- Participate in focused and sustained professional development that implements, nurtures, and sustains research-based learning and teaching.
  - Provide focused and comprehensive instructional leadership.
  - Model effective learning strategies while participating in professional development with staff.

Principal as the Face of the School

- Attend community events.
  - Promote the school.
  - Increase school involvement in the community.
- Ensure that steps are taken that guarantee improved educational experience for each student.
  - Improve the plight of students, which improves the perception of their parents.
  - Put structures in place that promote individualized instruction (mentoring, learning centers, remediation, etc.).
- Work to develop cooperative relationships between the school and the surrounding community.
  - Use the resources of the community.
  - Allow the community to use the school's resources.

Principal as a Manager

- Develop and manage the school budget.
  - Ensure that budget decisions reflect a commitment to the school's mission and vision.
- Select and evaluate instructional staff.
  - Make staff decisions based on student and learning needs.
  - Evaluate teachers based on their ability to successfully fulfill the tenants of the school's mission and vision.
- Deal with discipline and attendance concerns.
- Provide a safe and orderly learning environment.
- Maintain accountability for an effective and aligned instructional program.
- Ensure compliance with state and federal mandates.

Most of an educational leader's time is spent managing the school. This requires that the principal have the skills and competencies appropriate for businesses as well as the schoolhouse. But, contrary to popular opinion, the principal is not the CEO of the school. At best, the principal is the middle manager in a system of rules, regulations, and mandates from above—at the bottom of the pyramid of true policymakers.

Likewise, we expect much more of today's school superintendents. We no longer select them simply because of what they know about education, child development, teaching, or learning. They come to us from the ranks of business, the military, political power structures, or the legal profession. Frequently, they are managers not educators.

But command and control theory no longer works in education—not in the classroom or in the administration of schools. The days when principals and/or superintendents could order people to do things are over. Traditional top-down models of school leadership do not work in an educational environment where workers possess as much education and experiential knowledge as the nominal leader. Only collaboration will get the job done.

And the job remains daunting. We judge our principals and superintendents by a new bottom line: their students' academic success. In the 1960s, 1970s, and 1980s, we cared about equality of access and opportunity. Today, with the emphasis on higher standards, we focus on proficiency of achievement. We no longer expect school leaders to simply usher students through the grades at a level of learning that matches the population or its special needs. Each year, the numbers must show improvement. Politicians, business leaders, the media, the public and the parents expect excellence in every school district, school, and classroom.

School Leaders Are Made, Not Born

Scratch the surface of an excellent school and you will find an excellent leader. Conversely, look into a failing school and you will find weak leadership. According to research, leadership has a significant effect on student learning, second only to the effects of the quality of curriculum and teachers' instruction (Leithwood & Riehl, 2003).

Few professions train their leaders. We can think of two: business and the military. In the past education has looked to these as models. Granted, certain leadership qualities transcend those fields, and a few innovative businesses have redefined the corporate culture to draw on the skills and abilities of their workforce. In general, however, both business and the military use a *cascade* model where leadership flows from the well-trained, knowledgeable and educated cadre at the top to the less trained or educated workers at the bottom. As we have noted, education is not like that; classroom teachers are knowledgeable, well-educated professionals. Their leaders need a specific set of skills.

Often, we select our principals from the ranks of good teachers, good classroom managers, or superior teacher mentors. Too often, we fail to consider the skills, attitudes, and characteristics essential to effective leadership—and especially instructional leadership. Likewise, many college and university programs that train educational leaders work with individuals who choose administrative programs. Not many leadership programs go into the field to identify potential educational leaders. There is a huge difference between managing a school and leading instruction. Few principals do both well.

And yet, we believe that America's schools can improve. We believe that with effective training, greater resources, and support through mentoring, principals and superintendents can lead the way. All across America, we find examples of excellence—leaders who firmly believe that *all* children can succeed, schools that effectively meet the needs of nontraditional learners, and educational communities that don't give up on their at-risk students.

This book focuses on these examples of excellence. To write the book, we sought out educational leaders whose schools have effectively met the challenges of America's new educational landscape. We asked them to describe the attitudes and practices that made the difference between at-risk and excellence. Their responses form the backbone of this book.

Chapter 2 sets the stage, defining who is at risk and why. Chapter 3 describes our approach and frames the discussion with an overview of the responses from practitioners. In Part II, we delve into the specific areas where these school leaders made a difference: student learning and achievement, school improvement, staff empowerment, parent and family involvement, and school and community collaboration. In Part III, we present a road map for the journey from at risk to excellence.

In Appendix I, we include the survey sent to educational leaders whose schools have effectively met the needs of nontraditional learners. In Appendix II, we present the names of those recipients and their schools who responded to the survey and whose leaders agreed to let us acknowledge them publicly.

Along with the nationwide survey, we drew from responses to an Alabama survey of high-poverty public schools that have overcome odds and stand out as high-achievement schools. Fittingly, the final Appendix brings their voices alive. As practitioners speak our closing lines, these torchbearer schools offer a beacon of hope for our journey.

Chapter Summary

Public schools in the 21st century face the increased challenges of global competition for jobs and qualified graduates. Our nation will find the key to academic success in every school where an energetic, qualified, and well-trained principal is capable of maximizing the varied talents found in the faculty and staff.

2

Who Is At Risk
and Why

*What does it mean to "eradicate illiteracy"? It gives the impression of
pulling out bad weeds. It's insulting. We don't need to eradicate illiteracy, but the injustice that produces it.*

Paolo Freire
Pedagogy of the Oppressed

Before we explore the ways effective school leaders address the needs of at-risk learners, we must clearly define what "at risk" means and what factors put a student "at risk." Although several definitions of at-risk exist, one widely accepted approach describes at-risk students as those who are in danger of not completing high school—that is, our nation's prospective dropouts. The factors that put students at risk of dropping out fall into broad and necessarily overlapping categories. We will look first at individual risk factors—personal characteristics, habits and experience; family situations; and peer and community relationships—and then address the factors over which school leaders probably have more direct influence.

Individual Risk Factors

Although educators have long struggled to pin down the root causes of the school dropout problem, they cannot overlook the fact that students drop out as individuals—one by one. Programs that seek to stem the tide need a way to identify those individuals for academic, behavioral, or social intervention. To do this, they rely on individual risk factors: student characteristics and/or measures of past academic performance that are thought to increase the likelihood of a student dropping out of school.

The long list of individual risk factors includes tardiness, chronic absenteeism, low socioeconomic status, physical or mental disability, negative family interactions, being part of a family on welfare, academic problems, speaking English as a second language, a sense of alienation and disengagement from school, and poor peer acceptance. It is helpful to categorize such a list into groups of risk factors that share some similarities.

Although numerous researchers have compiled and categorized lists of individual risk factors, the following box—a fusion of the work done by Gleason and Dynarski (2002), Kominski, Jamieson, and Martinez (2001), Kubik, Lytle, and Fulkerson (2004), and Lagana (2004)—focuses the discussion in three areas and lists several individual risk factors pertinent to each area.

Previous School Experience

- Absent 20 or more times during the previous school year
- Retained in at least one grade
- Low grades (Cs and Ds or below)
- Disciplinary problems or disruptive behavior
- Has attended five or more schools during a lifetime

Personal or Psychological Characteristics

- External locus of control (perceived or actual)
- Low self-esteem
- At least one disability
- Poor peer support
- Depression or other emotional problems
- Early sexual activity or promiscuity
- Substance abuse

Adult and Family Responsibilities

- Has a child
- Must work to help support the family

This list encompasses a large number of children. A bare majority, 54%, of children in the United States do not experience any significant risk factors. Approximately 46% of America's school-aged children, more than 24 million, have at least one personal risk factor, and 18% have, or will have, multiple risk factors during their life (Kominski et al., 2001).

Family Background and Cohesion

When children first come to school, their values essentially reflect the culture in their homes. If that differs from the school's culture, conflict may arise; a child may be punished or ridiculed for behaviors that parents value. Such situations marginalize the child's self-worth and tend to alienate the student from the school, compromising performance. This clash of cultures, and its effect on the child's attitude toward school, is likely to manifest itself to a much greater degree as the United States grows increasingly pluralistic. This makes cultural awareness an important component of school climate, a factor addressed later in the chapter.

Parental discipline, monitoring, concern, encouragement, and consistency have also been linked to academic achievement. Children whose parents consistently set high standards work harder and do better in school (Natriello & McDill, 1986). Additionally, an authoritative parenting style, characterized by warmth and concern coupled with clear rules and limits, has been shown to have a positive effect on academic achievement. Single mothers—the heads of households in more than 20% of U.S. families (Annie E. Casey Foundation, 2003)—tend to be too permissive (Dornbusch et al., 1987). Parenting that is too strict or too permissive has a negative effect on student achievement (Dornbusch et al., 1987). In addition, poor parent–child relationships often culminate in the child having weak bonds to society as a whole, which makes the children more likely to deviate from societal norms. Such children are far more likely to drop out of school. The single-parent issue is discussed prominently in research concerning the at-risk learner; however, in many cases it is coupled with another risk factor: poverty.

Demographic studies reveal ample reason to couple single parent households and poverty in any discussion of individual risk factors. Families headed by a single mother are approximately five times more likely to live in poverty than families headed by two parents. The situation is even direr for families headed by a single black female. Such families are nearly seven times as likely to live in poverty; fully 64.5% of the families headed by single black females in the 18- to 24-year-old age group live below the poverty level (U.S. Census Bureau, 2004, Table POV-04).

Many studies have determined that poverty has a debilitating effect on a child's achievement level. Children of poverty begin school less prepared and consistently have poorer math and reading skills than students from families above the poverty line. In 2000 students who lived in families with incomes in the lowest 20% of all family incomes nationally were six times as likely to drop out of school as students who lived in families whose incomes were in the top 20% of the income distribution (National Center for Educational Statistics, 2001).

Family Background and Cohesion
1. Single-parent home
2. Family receives public assistance
3. Neither parent nor guardian is employed
4. Primary language of the family is not English
5. A sibling has dropped out of school
6. Parent(s) did not graduate from high school

School Experience

In a 2005 address to the Alabama State University Dropout Prevention Conference, Franklin Schargel suggested that there is no such thing as a high school dropout; it is more likely a case of *dim-out* over time. Individuals who drop out of high school start to flicker warning signals as early as first grade. A recent study of dropouts in Baltimore City Public Schools supports Schargel's argument. In that study, Alexander, Entwisle, and Kabbani (2001) found that dropouts had on average 60% more absences in the first grade than did graduates, 134% more absences in middle school, and 247% more by ninth grade. For most at-risk learners, dropping out is likely not a spur-of-the-moment decision. Consequently, school experiences could play a major role in their decision-making processes.

Researchers have shown that young people exposed to several risk factors simultaneously tend to experience learning and behavioral problems (Somers & Piliawsky 2004). There appears to be a direct link between those problem behaviors and motivation. The research also indicates that students who exhibit disruptive tendencies are extremely likely to experience academic difficulties. Disruptive behavior in young students interferes with their ability to interact successfully with teachers and peers and is predictive of several negative outcomes later in their academic careers. Those outcomes include academic difficulties, violent behavior, and dropping out of school (Laffey, Espinosa, Moore, & Lodree, 2003).

Peer and Psychological Characteristics

The literature extensively addresses two risk factors of a personal or psychological nature: peer support and substance use or abuse. Peer support, or a lack thereof, is identified as an important discriminator between high- and low-risk groups. At-risk learners who dropped out of school reported significantly less peer support than did high school graduates (Lagana, 2004). The lack of peer support is also a significant factor in the process of alienation and disengagement from school (McNeely, Nonnemaker, & Blum 2002). Equally important, negative peer group experiences in school tend to erode confidence levels and lead to many of the disruptive behaviors associated with dropping out of school (Win-Lin & Miu-Ling, 2003). Adolescents whose peers consistently participate in deviant behaviors are more likely to participate in those same behaviors, resulting in further alienation from the norms of the school setting.

Substance and alcohol abuse have played a prominent role in the research concerning individual risk factors and dropout rates. One third of the dropouts queried in Aloise-Young and Chavez's (2002) research reported that substance use and abuse contributed to their decision to drop out of school. Such percentages are fairly standard. A California study reported that 29.5% of the dropouts surveyed reported trying an illegal drug by age 12 years. In addition, the dropouts' weekly rates of alcohol, marijuana, and cocaine use were two, five, and ten times the rates of use by nondropouts (California Department of Alcohol and Drug Programs, 1995), respectively. The early initiation of drug and alcohol usage, by age 12 years in the California study, carries additional complications. Young adolescents who regularly use drugs or alcohol tend to be labeled *unconventional* or *nonconforming.* Such labels often lead to additional nonconformist or rebellious actions that reinforce antischool attitudes in the individual. This disengagement from school and its norms puts adolescents further at risk by forcing them to make more decisions on their own, without the benefit of adult input. Such situations make the disengaged youth much less likely to successfully complete adolescent phases of development, such as high school graduation, and much more likely to find themselves prematurely in adult roles that they cannot handle effectively (McCluskey, Krohn, Lizotte, & Rodriguez, 2002).

Fortunately, the obverse situation appears to be equally true. Swaim, Beauvais, Chavez, and Oetting (1997) found students in good standing with their schools less likely to experiment with illegal substances at an early age and far more likely to progress through traditional adolescent phases of development. In light of this study, we must question whether early onset of drug experimentation causes disengagement from school and its accompanying propensity for dropping out or disengagement from school leads to early onset of drug experimentation.

Individual Risk Factors Only Take Us So Far

A myriad of factors can put students at risk of dropping out of school. However, no single individual risk factor is rigidly deterministic. Not all youngsters from poor backgrounds drop out of school; not all students who experience disciplinary problems fail to graduate. Many children overcome their disadvantages and defy the demographic odds. This has led some to argue that all children should be able to do the same (Rothstein, 2004). Such arguments are specious at best. Not all smokers die of lung cancer nor all heavy drinkers of cirrhosis of the liver; but we recognize those outcomes as a distinct possibility. We must take the same approach with educational risk factors.

However, the factors traditionally used to identify children at risk have proven of limited use in predicting exactly who might drop out. The number of students who could be considered at risk further complicates the situation. By the year 2020, more children in the United States will be living in circumstances historically thought of as putting them at risk of school failure than will not (Sarason, 1995). At that point, leaders cannot rely solely on individual risk factors to set priorities for meeting their students' needs. They must take other avenues of approach.

A Better Focus for Schools

Evidence shows that we can define the characteristics of an effective school. Unfortunately, we do not find them in all schools—or even in enough schools. The increase in the number of private schools in this country, coupled with the dramatic rise in the number of students schooled at home, attests to this. But students who choose those options leave in search of a better education. The at-risk students who drop out of our public schools offer a more bitter indictment of a system that, over time, has failed them.

But our public schools can do better. Research indicates that early intervention can keep students from becoming academically at risk (Sapp & Farrell, 1994). The fact that efforts concentrating on individual risk factors have made little headway against the dropout problem since 1990 suggests that schools would do much better to focus on aspects they can influence directly: *climate and culture, school connectedness, school safety, attendance,* and *school achievement.*

Climate and Culture

Although we discuss climate and culture as a single separate factor here, they have enormous influence over the other four school-wide factors. Some studies have indicated that a school's primary path to addressing at-risk learners is to develop a more positive school climate and culture (Davenport & Anderson, 2002).

Multitudinous variables can have an impact on school climate and culture. Chief among these are the quality of teaching and the organization of academic programs. Research has indicated a significant relationship between high dropout rates and exposure to unorganized academic programs and poor teaching. Teaching and academic shortcomings lead to faculty and student morale problems that can poison a school's climate and culture (Duttweiler, 1995). By extension, those morale problems can dim a student's motivation to stay in school. That was the case in Sexton's (1985) study, in which students who transferred from schools with a high dropout rate to schools with a low dropout rate showed an increased tendency to stay in school. Sexton noted that climate and culture were almost always more positive in the schools with low dropout rates.

Teachers and how they teach play a major role in students' perception of a school's climate and culture. Empirical evidence suggests that schools can greatly influence a student's feelings of belonging at school and that teachers are vital to the development of a climate and culture that keeps students in school (Carter, 2001; Eccles, Midgefield, & Wigfield, 1993). A leading reason motivating at-risk students to stay in school is that they want to please those in authority (Kortering, Konold, & Glutting, 1998). Several studies have found that a lack of encouragement from teachers and administrators greatly influences a child's decision to drop out of school (Jordan, Lara, & McPartland, 1996; Kasen & Cohen, 1998; Martin, 1995). When dropouts were queried about their teachers, most reported poor-quality teachers who cared little about the students' well being. They also described their teachers as unfriendly and unapproachable (Engel, 1994; Wing-Lin & Miu-Ling, 2003). Such a disconnected relationship with teachers often leads students to perceive schools as cold and uncaring (Croninger & Lee, 2001). Those who strive to develop a healthy school climate and culture that more completely meets the needs of the at-risk learner should start by targeting teacher behavior.

School Connectedness

A positive school climate and culture enhances the second crucial school-wide domain: school connectedness. The concern about a lack of school connectedness as a factor in the dropout equation is not new. In the late 1950s, a study of 73 schools in Iowa, jointly conducted by the Iowa State Department of Public Education and the University of Iowa's College of Education, revealed a strong correlation between a lack of participation in school activities and dropping out of school (Hoyt & Van Dyke, 1958). Several more recent studies have yielded similar outcomes (Eccles, Early, Frasier, Belansky, & McCarthy, 1997; Resnik et al., 1997; Sprague & Nishioka, 2004; Steinberg, 1996). Students at risk of dropping out of school report disengagement characterized by a lack of participation in extracurricular activities, a feeling that they do not belong in the school, and a sense that school does not offer them a proper return on their investment of time and effort (Fuller & Sabatino, 1996; Hunt et al., 2002; Janosz et al., 1997; Woods, 1995). In the recent study commissioned by the Bill and Melinda Gates Foundation, *The Silent Epidemic, Perspectives of High School Dropouts* (March 2006), nearly half (47%) of respondents indicated that a major reason for their dropping out of school was that classes were not interesting.

Students are unlikely to feel connected to a school if the culture, climate, and social environment do not meet their developmental needs (McNeely et al., 2002). One of those is the need for relationships. Research reveals that socializing with peers is one of the five primary factors that motivate a child in school (Kortering et al., 1998). It also reinforces the premise that students who find relationships in a school, whether with peers or adults, feel more connected to that school and are more likely to overcome the risk factors with which they are saddled.

The fact that relationships with teachers and other adults increase the feeling of school connectedness is of particular import with minority children. Traditionally, one focus of public schools has been to assimilate all cultures into the American norm and, in doing so, to virtually overlook the importance of the minority students' home culture (Montecel et al., 2004). This often led to an institutionalized alienation that all but guaranteed an early exodus of minority children (Vanderslice, 2004). The disconnection that minority children feel from public schools has often been exacerbated by the mindset of their teachers. Research on teacher attitudes reveals that many view diversity of student backgrounds as a problem rather than an asset; many have negative attitudes about cultures and ethnic groups different from their own (Law & Lane, 1987; Paine 1989). Recognizing that a major facet of school connectedness is the relationships that students form with their teachers (Anderman & Maehr, 1994), a critical goal of any program to address the needs of the at-risk learner must be to strengthen the connections between teachers and all of their students.

School Safety

Individuals, whether adolescent or adult, tend to leave places where they do not feel safe (Dweyer, Osher, & Warger, 1998). That statement alone reinforces the critical nature of school safety. Furthermore, safety constitutes a cornerstone of a positive school climate (Magdol, 1998). Unfortunately, statistics underscore the fact that many schools are not safe; nationwide, 3 million students and teachers are crime victims each month (Miller, Fitch, & Marshall, 2003). Equally compelling statistics indicate that a safe and orderly school environment can positively affect the dropout rate (Woods, 1995). Anecdotal evidence leads to the same conclusion. In 1991 the Chicago Vocational School, a school of more than 2700 students, was reorganized into eight smaller schools, with an emphasis on positive school climates and safety. School size and increased connectedness played a role in the change, but students and teachers noted that the increased feeling of school safety was vital in trimming the dropout rate from more than 70% to less than 10% (Pascopella 1995).

Although surveys of school dropouts have indicated that safety, or the lack thereof, played a role in their decision to leave school, it should be noted that dropouts were also highly critical of what they saw as unfair and arbitrary discipline (Druian & Butler, 2001).

Attendance

Many have described dropping out as a process of disengagement marked by increased tardiness and decreased attendance—a process that continues until one day the student just stops coming to school. Schools and systems that actively enforce attendance policies to forestall this tend to be more effective in meeting the needs of the at-risk student and reducing their dropout population (Morris, 1994). Although attendance is an individual issue, school policy and attitudes toward attendance are not. Schools that effectively address attendance issues tend to have high school-wide attendance rates.

Academic Achievement

A lack of academic achievement has been identified as another factor in the at-risk student's decision to leave school early. One reason given is that failure results in alienation from school and increases the impetus to leave. Although academic achievement has traditionally been seen as an individual concern, research indicates that a relevant curriculum that is compellingly interesting can raise the achievement levels of all students (Barr & Parrett 1997; Castle 1994).

Relevance matters particularly to students who are struggling. They need to see the promise of a return for their increased input of time and effort (Schargel & Smink, 2001) or they are more likely to give up. Illich (1970) stated that learning results from "unhampered participation in a meaningful setting." Unfortunately, the same students who would benefit most from an interactive, truly meaningful curriculum are the ones most often deluged with workbooks to fill out and worksheets to complete. Such practices virtually preclude real engagement—a particularly unacceptable outcome in light of research showing that at-risk learners, even those with behavior problems, substantially improve in all aspects of their academics when presented with an appropriate and mentally stimulating curriculum (Lewis & Sugai, 1999).

Schools can substantially boost overall student achievement by providing a stimulating learning environment. The literature suggests a correlation between higher dropout rates and lower school-wide achievement, as measured by graduation exam percentages and standardized test scores. This should put creating a stimulating learning environment that promotes academic achievement high on the list of strategies to address the needs of at-risk learners.

> **School-Caused Risk Factors**
> - Ineffective discipline system
> - Overburdened school counselors
> - Negative school climate
> - Retention and/or suspensions used to control discipline, rather than addressing causes
> - Disregarding student learning styles
> - Passive instructional strategies
> - Lack of relevant curriculum
> - Low expectations of student achievement
> - Fear of school violence

Conclusion

The knowledge base explicitly describes the severe plight of the at-risk learner in America's public schools. Numerous studies have sought to illuminate the reasons why the dropout problem persists and identify objective ways to fight it. Still, the national dropout rate remains in the 11% range, and far higher for minorities.

However, the same studies that illuminate the plight of the at-risk learner should also invigorate the leaders responsible for their education. That research extols the benefits of a positive climate and culture. It underscores the need for at-risk learners to develop positive relationships with both peers and adults in the school setting. It reinforces the importance of a sound curriculum and a stimulating learning environment. It also highlights the need for schools to be safe for and accepting of the at-risk learner. Responsibility for working toward these goals falls squarely on the shoulders of the school's leaders.

Chapter Summary

The factors that put students at risk of dropping out fall into broad and necessarily overlapping categories. Individual risk factors include certain personal characteristics, habits, and experience; family situations; and peer and community relationships. Factors that school leaders can more directly influence include school climate and culture, school connectedness, school safety, attendance, and school achievement.

3

Defining the Focus: Practitioners Speak

What the best and wisest parent wants for his own child, that must a democracy want for all its children. Anything less is a diminution of the society.

John Dewey
Democracy and Education

Learning From Success

How We Identified Schools

To write this book, we asked *successful educational leaders* who deal with at-risk students about their attitudes and practices. We found them at successful schools and programs identified by the National Association of Secondary School Principals, the National Association of Elementary School Principals, the National Dropout Prevention Center at Clemson University, The Education Trust, the U.S. Department of Education's Blue Ribbon Schools program, a variety of state education departments, and the National Educational Resource Centers. Some schools offer recovery programs for students who have already left school and decided to come back.

We distributed more than 200 surveys to schools across the country; leaders from 19 different states responded. Some preferred to remain anonymous; most have given us permission to publish their contact information (see Appendix III). The schools highlighted here serve students ranging from kindergarten through high school. One community-based organization replied to the survey; we also heard from a parochial school, some charter schools, magnet schools, alternative schools as well as traditional schools. A friend in Australia asked to be part of our survey group. The remaining schools represent a cross-section of America. The surveys went to schools in large and small cities as well as rural and suburban areas. We made site visits to a number of schools to verify and validate the information we received.

How We Measured Success

The schools we identified as successful had to raise both academic achievement and graduation rates. Although we were interested in those schools that lowered their dropout rate, that criterion does not sort out schools that may have encouraged students to leave school to raise achievement statistics. Many of these schools are the *schools of last resort*, taking students who had left their *home* school, were extremely at risk, or even attending school as opposed to becoming part of the judicial system.

We assumed that the 23 schools we visited would show similarities in approach and attitude, and that proved to be true. However, the most striking characteristic found at all schools was their complete commitment to the educational process and the wellbeing of their students. Although each school approaches the task of educating young people in its own way, that shared commitment yields several major commonalities. The professional educators in these schools focus on student learning and achievement, school improvement, staff empowerment, parent and family involvement, and school–community collaboration.

Student Learning

In regard to the growth of the mind, we should set our goals very, very high, because we know that most people are capable of much more than they do or are.

Seymour B. Sarason,
Yale University

The schools in this study set high expectations for *all* students. However, many schools do the same without attaining similar levels of success. What sets these schools apart is that their goals are both tangible and measurable. *Maximize the learning potential of all students* is a laudable objective, but patently immeasurable. These schools strive to improve certain skills, by certain percentages, in specific periods of time. Such goals allow them opportunities to celebrate successes, which they do often, or objectively assess where they have failed and chart a new course.

In addition, the goals of the schools are discussed freely within the faculty and with the students. When we asked a principal in one struggling school whether she discussed test results with her students, she answered, "No, I don't want to hurt their feelings." Such an attitude clearly overlooks the truth of the matter: The students already know how they do on achievement tests and whether they are reaching the school's goals or falling short. Choosing not to discuss assessments openly and honestly with the student body does the students a disservice and compromises the faculty's credibility with their students. Successful schools clearly communicate school goals, more often than not have them posted in hallways and classrooms, and use any progress toward their goals as motivation for further improvement.

The schools also jointly develop a focused mission to improve student achievement, along with a vision of the school, curriculum, and instructional practices that makes higher achievement possible. In doing so, the schools always focus on providing the type of educational experiences that result in higher student achievement.

School Improvement

Because these schools place so much emphasis on student learning, it is not surprising that their school improvement initiatives all rest squarely on increasing student achievement. The schools recognize and encourage good instructional practices that motivate students and increase academic achievement by implementing structures that support good instructional practice. Those structures act as physical manifestations of theoretical *school beliefs*. For example, in the schools that state in their beliefs that "all students can learn," we invariably saw mentoring and remediation programs in place. Schools that truly believe all students can learn also understand that struggling students simply need additional help, which mentoring or remediation can provide.

The schools identified for this book also use data to guide school and classroom practices to increase student improvement. Student achievement should drive all schools, and it plays a major role at these schools. To determine how effectively they are addressing student needs, the schools use student assessment extensively. What differentiates the schools outlined here from many others is the amount of time they spend analyzing their assessment data and the extent to which they discuss that data with their students.

One principal stated, "Because of the amount of analysis of student data that we do, our teachers can allow their students to guide the instruction because it is based on student needs." Another responded that the school maintains "systematic, job-embedded training that includes regularly scheduled data meetings"; furthermore, the "teachers are required to keep progress-monitoring booklets on each student." Grade-level and staff meetings held solely for the purpose of discussing student data are also a common occurrence. Simply put, the extensive analysis of student achievement data conducted by these schools allows them to make decisions that impact instruction from a position of knowledge rather than a position of ignorance. Informed decision making is *the* key to school improvement.

Staff Empowerment

> *Teachers who chose the path of teacher leadership become owners and investors in their schools, rather than mere tenants.*
>
> Roland S. Barth, Founder,
> Harvard Principal Center

It is appropriate to point out that most principals who contributed to this book used the term *family or extended family* at some point when discussing their staff and faculty. Such a sense of community and shared responsibility was palpable in all the schools we visited, and the benefits of such an attitude were evident wherever we looked.

Each principal made a point of attributing the school's success directly to its personnel. Each also emphasized that their faculties are filled with leaders who see *all* students as *their* students and who seek to work with other teachers to benefit everyone. Such individuals truly take ownership in the educational process. These environments epitomize the concept of learning communities where the students are the ultimate benefactors.

Family Involvement

The schools in this study make parents partners in their child's education, creating structures for parents to cooperate with the administration and the staff. Most of the schools schedule multiple social events to provide parents with enjoyable, low-stress experiences that will make them more comfortable and feel more welcomed in the building. Such events are important; research indicates that more often than not, the parents of at-risk children did not have positive experiences in school themselves. It is unreasonable to expect parents to value an educational system that did not value them. Consequently, social events such as the monthly parent breakfasts conducted at Saltillo Elementary School are vital to building parental involvement in the school.

The schools we highlight understand that they cannot change the homes that students come from but, by including parents in the educational process, they can influence the conversation in those homes. Since Oak Mountain Intermediate School began including parent volunteers in all aspects of school life, to include a parent liaison on all school committees, the school has seen a dramatic increase in parental support. Such support almost always leads to increased student attendance and a corresponding increase in student achievement.

School–Community Collaboration

Power in organization is the capacity generated by relationships.

Margaret Wheatley

Schools cannot exist in a vacuum separate and distinct from the surrounding community. Much like a principal who fails to use the strengths of the faculty, a school that does not seek out and make use of the strengths found in the community it serves is doomed to fail. The need is especially pronounced in schools tasked with educating the poor. The perception lingers in many communities, especially those serving poor neighborhoods, that schools exist as islands and care little about educating their children.

Fortunately, the schools featured in this book have put into place numerous structures to ensure that they are not viewed as insular. Several schools indicated that they have active public relations committees tasked with maintaining open and healthy lines of communication between school and community. Committees actively disseminate positive news about their school. As the principal at Dutton Elementary School, Dale Hancock, stated, "Everyone wants to be associated with a winner, so we make sure everyone hears the good news about our school." The structures that these schools establish allow them to proactively strengthen and secure the bond they have with their community. That bond makes their communities equally proactive in seeking ways to help. Such a symbiotic relationship ultimately results in a school that can more effectively meet the needs and raise the achievement of its students.

Chapter Summary

What are the common factors that make schools successful in dealing with at-risk learners? Our instructional leaders consistently focused on five areas:

1. Student learning and achievement
2. School improvement
3. Staff empowerment
4. Family involvement
5. School–community collaboration

Part II

Focus on What Really Matters

4

Student Learning
and Achievement

Most learning is not the result of instruction. It is rather the result of unhampered participation in a meaningful setting.

Ivan Illich

Illich's assertion underscores the importance of leadership in the development of schools that address the needs of all learners. Every adult in the school has responsibility for ensuring that classrooms are indeed meaningful settings. Above all, the principal must provide the resources and support teachers need to make every classroom meaningful to the students. And the principal and school leadership team must impress on the adults in the building that every interaction matters. One can never tell when each child is most ready to learn. Schools cannot afford to waste a valuable teaching opportunity, whenever it occurs.

Not only must leaders provide the tools and support necessary to succeed, they must set the stage for appropriate use of those tools. It is one thing to supply technological resources; it is quite another to be sure teachers know how to use them and are willing to do so.

Start With the Physical Setting

> Learning must take place in an environment that is conducive to learning. The very first thing we did was bring life to our vision by renovating the building. Schools should be child-centered and friendly to all who enter.
> *Patricia Kornegay*, Highland Avenue Elementary School

> The first year we painted in bright colors, cleaned doors and windows and planted trees. We placed park benches in the hallways with ficus trees. We made our school a more inviting place to learn.
> *Dale Hancock*, Dutton School

Leaders find it much easier to create a meaningful setting in a school to which students and adults enjoy coming. Numerous studies have addressed the effect of environment on mood and motivation; the schools in this study clearly get it right. For at-risk students, many of whom view their school as cold and uncaring, a positive and inviting atmosphere is vital. For all students, a vibrant, clean, and colorful physical environment sends a clear signal that the faculty and staff take pride in the school and its mission.

In our visits to 23 of the schools that contributed to this book, we noticed right away that the students and the faculty took pride in their school facilities. We saw vibrant colors everywhere. Examples of student work adorned the hallways, bulletin boards, and every classroom. Although it is the norm in many places, we could not see any graffiti. Most importantly, we found each school exceptionally clean.

The principals in these schools universally described cleanliness as an outward expression of personal and professional pride. Keeping their schools clean paved the way for providing every student with a more appropriate learning environment. This held true particularly for students who cannot count on cleanliness and order in their home environments. At George Hall Elementary School in inner-city Mobile, staff and faculty worked long hours over the summer to clean, paint, and organize their space. Terri Tomlinson, the principal, stated, "It was all worthwhile when we saw the smiles on the parents' and students' faces the first day of school." Seven months later, we found the school and the smiles still shining.

The principals agreed that the easiest way to set off toward a better school is to change the physical environment. They may have limited funds to paint or decorate, but resourceful leaders can come up with plenty of the *elbow grease* needed to clear away clutter and grime. Once the school and grounds are clean, the school must implement a systematic approach to keeping them that way. Little things like tidying up break areas *before* the break starts and cleaning the cafeteria *before* each meal make a big difference. Students and adults alike find it much easier to throw the 20th scrap of paper on the ground than the first. We often overlook the physical environment or consider it ancillary to the learning process, but it can be crucial to students' attitudes and pivotal to their achievement.

Students should feel connected to their schools. To foster this connection, effective schools develop a welcoming environment. This can start with something as simple as having someone at the front door of the school and the classroom to welcome and greet students, which creates an environment of safety and friendship rather than hostility and coldness.

The physical environment makes a big difference to student attitudes and, consequently, to student achievement. A clean, inviting, and stable learning environment underpins a healthy school as well as any systemic approach to addressing the needs of the at-risk learner.

Encourage the Bold Reach

> The "hidden curriculum" must be addressed before any other learning can occur.
>
> *Larry Sholes*, Attucks Alternative Academy

The first step toward systematically addressing the needs of at-risk students is to closely inspect the school's curriculum from both a technical and a nontechnical perspective. Technically, a curriculum consists of the subjects to be taught and the framework within which they are taught. From a nontechnical perspective, the curriculum includes the school and instructor philosophies, school histories, and school culture. All these influence decisions about which aspects of the technical curriculum teachers emphasize. From a holistic standpoint, the true curriculum encompasses *what* is taught, and *how*, and *why*. Therein lies the challenge.

Here is a wonderful exercise to do with faculty members:

Ask a few to come forward, raise their hands, and touch the wall. Place painter's tape to mark where each hand touched the wall. Now, tell the volunteers that you think they can reach higher. Ask them to try again and see if they can reach a higher point on the wall. Mark this higher point with another piece of painter's tape. Ask the audience if they believe they could help the volunteers reach even higher. Invite a few to come and assist. Place yet another piece of tape at each higher mark. Now ask the audience to discuss what happened, and relate the process to improving student achievement.

Students recognize a dumbed-down curriculum. They see it as signaling the belief that they cannot do any better, and they react accordingly. Such messages gnaw away at the motivation and confidence of struggling students. Walk into any kindergarten classroom in the nation and look at the joy on the children's faces. Then enter a middle or high school classroom and look around. What happened to those happy kindergartners? How much of the change in demeanor comes from exposure to learning environments that fail to support their learning and drain the excitement out of them?

Our three "R's" are rigor, relevance, and relationships.
Larry Sholes, Attucks Alternative Academy

We eliminated low-level courses but created many supports and safety nets for students.
David Besile, R. B. Stall High School

The successful schools highlighted in this book share a strong commitment to high expectations for both students and teachers. One of the major motivations of today's students is pleasing authority (Kortering, Konold, & Glutting, 1998). This suggests that clearly explaining and modeling high expectations yields stronger performance. Several studies have also found that a lack of encouragement from teachers and administrators plays a major role in a child's decision to give up and eventually drop out of school (Jordan, Lara, & McPartland, 1996; Kasen & Cohen, 1998; Martin 1995). The school leader must make sure school and classroom cultures send the clear message that every student is expected to achieve at high levels.

One major problem associated with the high-stakes testing environment found in today's schools is its effect on actual learning. No real learning can occur in the absence of mistakes. Most scientists know full well that failure is the foundation on which innovation is built. In every school, both teachers and students must be encouraged to take intellectual risks for the sake of improvement. They must also be supported when they fail and prompted to reflect on what they could have done differently. Only in such an environment can true innovation pave the way for monumental progress.

> We encourage intellectual risk-taking among both teachers and students.
> *Linda Maxwell*, Oak Mountain Intermediate School

> We encourage risk-taking and creative approaches to education.
> *Judy Knotts*, St. Gabriel's Catholic School

> Achievement precedes behavior change: Academic success breeds behavioral success, and significant improvement is noted toward the end of the first grading period in the program.
> *Elmer Magyar*, New Directions Alternative Education Center

In a study of high-poverty, high-performing schools in Alabama, principals were nearly unanimous in their belief that good teaching minimizes disciplinary problems. The consensus was that no one wants to leave or be removed from an environment in which they are engaged and find enjoyment or self-fulfillment. Principals stated that students with discipline problems are generally the same students with academic problems, and resolving the academic difficulties generally mitigated the disciplinary problems as well. Several other studies echo these findings (Laffey, Espinosa, Moore, & Lodree, 2003; Somers & Piliawsky, 2004).

Establish Innovative Programs

Even in a high-stakes testing environment, truly innovative programs create successes against the apparent odds. However, it must also be noted that programs we listed were put in place to address needs not met by standard, needs identified through data analysis.

> Single-gender classes have been particularly beneficial for male at-risk students.
> *Lee Mansell*, Foley Intermediate School

> School can take many forms and some of them do not include brick and mortar. We are running an "evening opportunity school" and offer courses over the web for credit and recovery.
> *Richard Varrati*, New Philadelphia City Schools

Embrace the Data

> We utilize up-to-date practices such as interactive computer technologies (ICT), student contracts, and negotiated curriculums with students.
>
> *Cliff Downey*, Mooroopna Park Primary School

> Student achievement was not the burning issue. We knew our students could learn. We focused on student engagement based on daily discussions of data.
>
> *Terri Tomlinson*, George Hall Elementary School

> I keep score. I am constantly looking at data and trying to analyze student and teacher performance. I post data periodically to emphasize what is important. "What gets measured gets done."
>
> *Dale Hancock*, Dutton School

> We ensure the use of data in all classrooms by students, ensuring that they are self-monitoring their progress and participating as active learners.
>
> *Larry Sholes*, Attucks Alternative Academy

For years, educational leaders have collected data and dutifully forwarded it to central offices and state departments of education without taking the time to analyze what they collected. Consequently, when the No Child Left Behind Act necessitated an analysis of the data and dissemination of that analysis, many educators were caught off guard. Their surprise suggested that many schools were making decisions based on subjective rather than objective reasoning. That practice is no longer acceptable. Schools must analyze their own data and discuss the findings among both the faculty and the student body. It is unfair to expect improvement from students without giving them an objective measure of where they started. The same is true of teachers. The principals who contributed to this study firmly believe that data analysis underpins and guides their campaigns to meet the needs of all students.

Provide Informed Support

> What gets monitored gets done. I complete a "target setting" activity with each teacher where we set a target and develop strategies to improve the achievement of each student.
>
> *Deborah Lazio*, Chester Dewey School #14

The nationwide emphasis on high-stakes standardized testing makes it vitally important for school leaders to ensure that what is taught aligns with what is tested. Those who neglect this alignment of their schools put their students at risk of failure. This simply exacerbates the problem. Educational leaders at the state level regularly review state standards and courses of study to make sure they are aligned with national requirements. Fourteen of the principals who contributed to this book emphasized the importance of aligning school practice to state and national standards.

> Everyone identifies the at-risk learner. We work hard to identify their interferences to learning. Then we define their support system.
>
> *Dale Hancock*, Dutton School

> We have studied Dufour's book *Whatever It Takes* and developed and implemented our own pyramid of interventions. That pyramid has provided the basis for informed intervention with students who are at risk of failing.
>
> *Terri Tomlinson*, George Hall Elementary School

> We develop support plans at our monthly roundtable meetings that include social services, police department, DYS, mental health agencies, and so forth.
>
> *Milton Public Schools*

> We are in the early stages of looking at students through the lens of neuro-developmental constructs and are continuing staff development to improve our skills in supporting all children.
>
> *Linda Welch*, Whittier School

> We have conducted training in specific strategies that work with low-performing students, concentrating on Piaget's concrete operations stage.
>
> *Linda Maxwell*, Oak Mountain Intermediate School

Once assured that instruction is properly aligned with standards, the instructional leader must then endeavor to provide informed support to the students. That support can start from many actions, with diagnostic testing one of the most popular. One particularly telling example stems from the use of the ABLE II diagnostic test in a southeastern Alabama alternative school. When students who were struggling in math took the test, it revealed that their mathematical computation skills were consistently 2 to 3 years behind their problem-solving abilities. In response, the school began a remediation program that stressed multiplication and division skills. Math achievement levels improved almost immediately.

Diagnostic testing is not the only way to determine the type and extent of support needed. The principals surveyed supplied many examples of approaches to providing informed support for at-risk learners. We highlight some of them here and throughout the chapter.

Clearly, efforts to boost the academic achievement of at-risk students rely on boosting their motivation. However, leaders must base their actions on objective measures. This starts with taking stock of the current situation. To adequately and appropriately address situations that put students at risk, the educational leader must answer the following questions:

◆ How many at-risk students are enrolled in the school/district?

◆ What do demographic data about our school/district indicate about the number of at-risk students in the future?

◆ What current school/district programs and policies create special problems for at-risk children and youth?

◆ What resources are available in the school/district and in the community to meet the needs of at-risk students?

◆ How can we involve families of at-risk students in their educational achievement?

◆ How can partnerships with businesses or colleges and universities improve educational opportunities for at-risk students?

The answers to these questions cannot be intuitive. They must be based on objective data.

The increased achievement demands of state departments of education and the federal government have caused schools to intensify their efforts to raise academic achievement for all students. Traditionally, professionals focused on improving instruction, believing that this would lead to stronger achievement. Supervisors measured improvement in terms of lesson plans, motivations, and pivotal questions. Although these efforts yielded some improvement, they placed too much emphasis on the teaching and not enough on the learning.

Use Assessment as a Guide

We must develop a broader and more relevant system of assessment designed to measure the varied abilities that contribute to success in the *real world*. Measuring school performance solely against a preconceived notion of what students need today trivializes the world that students enter tomorrow. We know that graduates will need a wider variety of skills than today's tests require. We know that students must work in teams, solve problems, and think creatively as individuals. Today's assessments fail to measure those capabilities.

> *Where assessment is educative, we hear classroom and hallway conversations that are different than those heard in schools that use traditional assessment methods. Students are no longer asking teachers, "Is that what you want?" or "Is this going to be on the test?" Instead, learning*

goals and standards are so clearly spelled out that students understand what they are expected to learn. Moreover, these goals and standards are spelled out in terms of performance so that students know how they are expected to demonstrate their learning.

Grant P. Wiggins
Co-Founder, Center on Learning,
Assessment, and School Culture

Dr. Myron Tribus, an innovative leader in fields such as engineering and management, insists, "The sole purpose of testing is to determine what to do next." Standardized tests given at the end of the school term with results produced over the spring break or summer simply measure success in mastering material or the failure to learn that material. The minute educators determine that a student is struggling to master the lessons of the day or week, they must develop an instructional *safety net*. That safety net can be Saturday remedial classes, a before- or after-school support program, a *lunch and learn* tutorial program or other assists. Waiting until the end of the term to *punish* failure is stupidity; holding students back to merely flounder for another year is insanity.

We offer credit recovery with NovaNet (an online interactive curriculum) and an Alternative Education Plan to each student that includes shared responsibility and personally set goals.

Elmer Magyer, New Directions, Alternative Education Center

Maximize Mentoring and Tutoring

If schools are to succeed with nontraditional learners, they must confront the problem of time constraints. They may choose to extend the school day, prolong the school year, or add summer programs. They should implement intensive reading and writing programs to facilitate student learning both in the school setting and the community (e.g., self-directed learning, service learning): classroom structure (e.g., multiage, multigrade). They can make use of community resources, such as the local YWCA to support learning.

Schools must make sure that students have the time, resources, and personnel to catch up if they haven't mastered reading and math skills and concepts. They may have students take additional math or reading classes every semester. Trained mentors can aid schools by coaching students in the skills they lack. This saves schools and communities money by reducing the number of students who later need special education or remedial classes.

Reduce Class Size

Smaller classes help personalize learning and allow youngsters to more easily relate to teachers. Tennessee's Project STAR (Student/Teacher Achievement Ratio) tracked 11,000 students randomly assigned in the early grades to regular classes (approximately 25 students), small classes (15 students), and regular classes with an instructional aide. Children in small classes outperformed those in regular ones, with or without an aide, and differences were still reflected years later. And an Educational Testing Service (ETS) study of fourth- and eighth-grade students found that math scores of inner-city fourth-graders in classes of fewer than 20 students were about three-quarters of a grade level ahead of those of their counterparts in larger classes (Jones, 1998).

Choose Technology for the Steak, Not the Sizzle

> Every teacher has a databank folder of PowerPoints, movies, and computer-based activities that our tech committee has pulled from the Internet to help them match their teaching to their students' needs.
>
> *LaVeral Graf*, W. C. Griggs Elementary School

Technology is a tool. Like all tools, if not used properly, it can do more harm than good. Schools can use technology effectively to vary and enrich instruction, but they must develop long-term plans to help classroom teachers make the best use of today's technologies. Teachers should not use computers mainly as electronic books; the bells and whistles don't add substance to teaching or learning, nor should they send students who complete their work early off to the machines to do *whatever*. Structured practical use of computers will provide enjoyment as well as provide increased learning.

Classrooms need not become *Monday at the movies*. Teachers can readily show snippets of movies as grabbers, and spend the rest of the class with students actively engaged. They can also take advantage of the hours students already spend in front of the TV after school. Teachers might have students write a review of what they watched (in English), determine who the leader in "Survivor" was (leadership), or evaluate the latest show on the Discovery Channel (for the sciences). This extends the structured learning environment and focus of the school day into the evening hours.

Model the Expected

Student perceptions of their performance do not always coincide with their instructors' views. We must create models that demonstrate for students what an *A* paper looks like. We should take the time to show them why the math problem or English paper does not meet the standard for a passing grade. Students must realize that they are responsible for the actions that will lead to their success. This awareness can be developed through a mutually agreed contract between students and the school.

Teach Time Management

> Intensive scheduling: one to two courses at a time for a nine-week period.
> *Elmer Magyer,* New Directions Alternative Education Center

> 75 percent of our at-risk students have ADD [attention deficit disorder]. We give them four-hour, four-week blocks of instruction. This means they have one homework, one test, and one textbook.
> *Mary Jo McLaughlin,* The Academy of Creative Education

It is a given that students *cram.* They postpone writing papers until the last minute. They fritter away study halls or other study opportunities. They study hardest for examinations as they ride the bus to school on the day of the test. Families and educators alike must take concrete steps to counteract these tendencies. They must designate and supervise opportunities for studying and doing research. Parents can structure a block of time and a quiet place for their child's focused learning. Educators should monitor study halls and the school library to ensure that students stick with productive work. Schools should establish designated areas for students to socialize, set apart from the environment and space maintained for those who want to study or do research.

Promote Clubs, Teams, and Groups

Effective schools are more than safe havens and citadels of learning; they must also be places where children enjoy themselves. To make that happen, schools should establish teams, clubs, groups, and special activities and deliberately encourage students to experience these organizations. Students actively involved in a school are less likely to leave it by dropping out.

Enrich Learning

We initiated IDM (Instructional Decision Making) and RTI (Response to Intervention) three years ago as an early intervention process for any student identified with areas of concern—academic, emotional/social, and/or behavioral. Early intervention is the key.

Pat Sievers and Julie Stoneburner, Ankeny Community School District

Effective schools and programs do not give students the option of failing. They watch for signs of faltering steps and respond right away. They anticipate obstacles and prepare students to approach them with the necessary tools and skills. They train students in how to take tests, study, and manage time. They enrich existing programs through the use of focused professional development. They provide stretch goals so that students can expand their horizons through offerings such as advanced placement classes and international baccalaureate programs. And they offer these opportunities to *all* students.

Provide Structure

In these turbulent times, schools provide the structure so many youngsters lack at home. They have taken on responsibilities normally associated with parental responsibilities: feeding children, teaching driver's education and swimming, and providing sexual education. At-risk learners need more structure than most. And the answer to this structure is not additional school suspensions.

We focus on student learning styles/needs to determine instruction. Our attitude is we will find ways of reaching every student.

Betty Warren, Huxford Elementary School

These schools realize that not all students learn effectively with an abstract approach to the teaching of essential skills, concepts, and content. Some students learn best through real-world applied concepts.

We know that most students have difficulty clearing the hurdle of going from eighth to ninth grade. Many schools report an upswing of students retained in ninth grade because they *weren't ready* to go on to high school. Visionary leaders redesign schools so that the teacher to student ratio is lower in the ninth grade. They also assign additional counselors so that learning and counseling is more personalized and students don't fall through the cracks. Unprepared ninth graders can take a double dose of language arts or mathematics if that is where the challenge lies.

Additional self-paced opportunities allow students to retake courses they have failed so that they can move on with their peers, avoid the stigma of being *left back* and reduce the likelihood of dropping out. If the objective is getting students to pass classes and graduate, the school must do everything possible to achieve this objective. Giving students extra help to meet higher standards shows them that the school and their teachers believe they can learn more challenging materials (Bottoms, 2001).

Counselors have the potential to directly aid the learning process. However, their caseload is very large (350–450 students is the norm). Schools should relieve them of dealing with some paperwork requirements, so they can spend more time counseling students and helping raise student achievement by focusing on the strengths and weaknesses students show in classes.

Unchallenged youngsters can be offered opportunities that engage them. They can be asked to teach classes in teams; develop lesson plans; prepare major research papers; or make oral presentations to parents, business groups, and politicians.

The leaders who contributed to writing this book insisted that engendering an internalized motivation to learn, in both the students and the adults in their schools, was pivotal to their success. Successfully motivating at-risk youth requires behaviors that reflect the following basic beliefs:

- ◆ All students are capable of learning when they are provided the academic and personal tools to succeed.
- ◆ Students are inherently motivated to learn; they learn to be unmotivated when they repeatedly fail.
- ◆ Learning requires taking intellectual risks. Classrooms should be safe places, physically and psychologically, where children and their teachers are given permission to take risks.
- ◆ All students have basic needs to belong, be competent, and influence what happens to them. Motivation to learn most often occurs when these basic needs are met.
- ◆ High self-esteem should not be a goal in itself but rather a result that comes with the mastery of challenging tasks.
- ◆ High motivation for learning in school most often occurs when adults treat students, and students treat each other and adults, with respect, trust, and dignity.

Chapter Summary

Illich's words, "Unhampered participation in a meaningful setting," encapsulate the fundamental needs of at-risk students. The challenge lies in determining what constitutes a meaningful setting and finding ways to provide it. The first step toward systematically addressing these needs is to closely inspect the school's curriculum. The successful schools highlighted in this book share high expectations for both students and teachers, underpinned by objective data. Effective schools analyze their own data and discuss the findings among both the faculty and the student body as an objective measure of starting points and progress. The data then guide the campaign to provide informed support to all students. Effective schools deploy a variety of innovative approaches and instruments to reach their goals.

5

School Improvement

In times of change, learners inherit the Earth, while the learned find themselves beautifully equipped to deal with a world that no longer exists.

Eric Hoffer

Times have changed, and schools have changed as well; but they have not kept pace with changes in society and the workplace. If we look at the school structure, we see it draws on the industrial model. Students march through their days like products on an assembly line. The school calendar still follows the farmer's year, with time off for planting and harvesting.

> The structure worked relatively well for the agricultural/industrial society it was designed to serve. It provided schooling for millions of immigrants, inculcated the skills and conformity need to staff assembly lines, and followed a calendar dictated by agricultural seasons. Aspiring teachers had to pass rigorous exams to enter teaching, teaching was a respected profession, and there was a surplus of highly qualified teachers. The students who entered the system had high standards set for them, parents pushed their children to excel, and most students were attentive to their teachers. *This structure, however, was designed to sort and select; it was never designed to provide quality education for all students* [emphasis added]. The kinds of reforms that emerged followed a strategy of intensification—continuing to do what has been done for years, but doing more of it and presumably doing it better. (Duttweiler, 1995)

Among the many myths coursing through the education community is that its structures are sacrosanct. Nothing could be farther from the truth. They do not possess permanent, timeless validity. The subjects taught, the class schedules, and the very makeup of schools have not always been what are today. Unlike the laws of nature, social institutions are functions of history and of specific times and places. Recognizing this simple fact opens a wealth of opportunities for reform.

Traditional teaching and learning techniques do not work with nontraditional learners. Therefore, if we wish to succeed with nontraditional students, we must change the teaching and learning process. Those who truly seek to address the needs of all children should not ask, "What can we do within the constraints of our current situation?" The question must simply be, "What must we do to get better?" The answers to and the implications of those two questions are far different. The kind of school improvement that usually necessary for growth cannot be viewed as incremental tinkering or polishing. Sometimes it must be an overhaul.

Furthermore, the structures in need of reform may be attitudinal as much as physical. The best schools are not places where students learn, but places where *everyone* learns. A culture where the adults are actively and enthusiastically learning is a culture where the students are learning as well. Therefore, school improvement rests squarely on the shoulders of school leaders. Before any substantive improvement can occur, the school leader must see the need for that improvement.

The answers to two simple questions can help any leader determine how gravely improvement is needed:

1. Does the intrinsic motivation of your students increase the longer they attend your school (Walsh & Sattes, 2000)?
2. Does the intrinsic motivation of your teachers increase the longer they work at in your school?

Those who cannot immediately answer "yes" to both questions have identified an unequivocal need for school improvement.

Those on the outside (business people, politicians, citizens) want instant improvement. They measure results in short time cycles. Even if a program works, it always takes a while to show pupil growth. We grow impatient to see positive results. But education in the United States took a long time to decline. It will not recover overnight.

Murphy's Law states that if anything can go wrong, it will. Many educators feel it was developed specifically to deal with education. What is predictable is that the unpredicted will take place. Things will take longer or shorter to happen. Materials and machinery will not arrive. Water will seep from the third floor to the first. Hurricanes will displace hundreds of thousands of children. Schools operate in a society that is constantly in flux. Ed Bales, formerly of Motorola University, once defined school change as "trying to change the tire on a car moving at 60 miles an hour." Inevitably, the effort to achieve change will include dealing with the contradictory, the uncontrollable, and the unexpected (Trubowitz, 1997).

A Culture of Change

You must recognize that evolution is necessary and advisable.
Elmer Magyar, New Directions, Alternative Education Center

Nowhere is change more prevalent than in schools. For students, each year subjects change, friends change, teachers change, and the stakes change. Leaders should create an environment that is friendly to change. Someone once said that the only one who desires change is a baby with a wet diaper—and even they fuss about it. Educators fear change no more than most. Although a school's culture is one of the hardest things to change, it is nonetheless always evolving. One can either guide the change or be a slave to it. A good leader guides the change.

School improvement takes place in the following circumstances:

◆ There is a leader to drive the process.
◆ People in the institution are no longer satisfied with the status quo.

- ◆ Either staff or the leader issues a call for school improvement.
- ◆ The group desiring change outnumbers those who want to continue down the existing road.

Resistance to Change

Educators often encounter the frustration of having changes suggested by people without experience in the field—people who neither understand their short- and long-term implications nor provide the funding to support the change. Some unsound programs have been *doomed to success*, surviving because of the amount of time, energy, and expense already invested. Other initiatives perform well when launched under outside grants; but even when those at the top acknowledge their efficacy, they do not maintain them with district funding when the grant monies cease to flow.

Seasoned principals and superintendents advance to higher office or move to school districts with higher salaries, better working conditions, and less micromanaging from school boards. The new leaders may not discover the backstory behind school or district programs, initiatives, and plans. They may lack the motivation to implement proposals they do not *own*. They may provide less support to sustain the momentum, or dilute the interest and attention given to ongoing change efforts.

Repeated often enough, such scenarios generate skepticism on the part of veteran professionals who have witnessed one short-lived program after another and watched the *flavor of the day* (or week or year) come and go. Like most of us, they value stability. They see the known as bearable, the unknown as forbidding. Little wonder they hesitate to embrace suggestions of change.

Peter Senge has commented that people don't resist change; they resist "being changed." So much of the change humans experience comes from forces over which they feel they have little or no control. Often, people are asked to change without any understanding of why. Many of life's changes mean giving up what is familiar for what is not. It stands to reason, then, that people learn to equate change with loss.

In a survey of educational practitioners, Duttweiler and Mutchler (1991) found eight major barriers to changing educators' traditional behavior:

1. *Fear of taking risks:* The lack of a cooperative goal structure and fear of reprisal slowed down the implementation of many change efforts.

2. *Fears of losing power:* School board members and administrators at all levels were apprehensive about losing power in any reform effort that included a redistribution of authority.

3. *Resistance to changing roles and responsibilities:* Both administrators and teachers were reluctant to forge different roles or accept new responsibilities. They were apathetic to changes, favored the status quo, or identified with traditional norms and roles.

4. *Lack of trust:* Mistrust cropped up at every level of the system and in every relational permutation.

5. *Lack of skills:* A lack of skills, particularly in working with groups and group decision making, was a critical barrier to successful change.

6. *Lack of definition and clarity in the change effort:* Survey respondents reported the lack of clear definition of the change effort itself, the strategies to be used to implement it, the boundaries of school authority, and the behaviors expected in new roles and responsibilities.

7. *Inadequate resources:* Educators identified a lack of resources or resource allocation as a serious barrier to change. They identified time as the most important and most inadequate resource.

8. *Lack of hierarchical support:* Respondents reported major problems resulting from the absence of full-system commitment to change, transience of personnel, inadequate communication, and conflicts with outside agencies.

Change is rarely comfortable and never easy. Meaningful change demands careful planning, coordination, collaboration, and understanding. And change in a community poses a greater challenge because it requires the buy-in of numerous individuals, some of whom firmly believe that the prospective change threatens their power and prestige. That is especially true in the school setting. Consequently, any principal attempting to improve a school must prepare to encounter resistance. If resistance does not occur, then the change was probably not worthwhile in the first place or, worse yet, those affected do not care enough to resist.

In his book *Paradigms: The Business of Discovering the Future,* Joel Barker (1993) explains resistance to change in this way:

> New paradigms put everyone practicing the old paradigm at great risk. The higher one's position, the greater the risk. The better you are at your paradigm, the more you have invested in it, and the more you have to lose by changing.

Research has indicated three primary reasons for resistance to change. With Barker's quote as a backdrop, it should come as no surprise that the first reason is emotional. When someone presents an emotional argument against the change, it is important for the leader to show empathy with the resister. Many times, those who balk fear the change and worry about their ability to master it. A useful response is to reinforce the simple fact that those who exemplified excellence in the old system will do the same in the new, and probably to a much greater degree.

The second main reason for resistance to change is intellectual. In such instances the leader should express understanding of the heel-dragger's stance, but juxtapose it with the prospective benefits of the change. This tactic grounds the discussion in logic. A well-planned change initiative will likely end up perceived in a positive light.

The third source of resistance emerges when the change is at odds with the resister's belief system. This is the most difficult situation to overcome. Thankfully, in the educational setting it is also the least encountered. The response to this type of resistance must include at least tacit acceptance of the resister's values, followed by a careful discussion of why the change is necessary.

Experience has shown that each of these responses effectively counters a particular type of resistance to change. However, none work as well as providing ample communication about the change up front and ensuring that any reservations are considered and addressed early on. Most resistance springs from ignorance of the change and all it entails. Sufficient communication can go a long way toward alleviating that ignorance.

The Messages of Resistance

Leaders who understand the reasons for resistance can counteract its effects. Listen to these balky staff members. How should the leader respond?

I don't know why he wants to start changing things. I just don't see the need to change from what we are currently doing."

Rather than dismissing such statements as laziness or negativity, acknowledge the human need to understand why old ways must yield to the new. Recognize that not all will agree at first; agreement comes much later, when those who must adapt see the change as beneficial.

"Why does he want us to change? I think he is up to no good."

When people equate change with loss, distrust is a normal by-product. Expect them to question your motives. Reassure them that they will have input into the process, and follow through with that promise. People who experience change as collaborative, at least in part, will feel more in control. Give them a voice whenever possible.

"How does she know this new thing will work? I know what I do now works."

Not all change is for the better. Give people the right to question change until they are convinced of its worth. Respect their healthy curiosity and a certain amount of *prove it* mentality. This may help you avoid taking the wrong path, or save face if things don't work out as you expected. But act with conviction and expect doubters to go along once it is clear the new way is better than the old.

"This too shall pass. I will just wait long enough, quietly continue what I do, and wait for this to go away."

Expect this attitude from a certain few whenever change is afoot. They may express it only among themselves, but it lurks nonetheless, rooted in long experience of educational initiatives that were much heralded, poorly implemented, and quietly forgotten. To enlist these veterans as agents for change, demonstrate that the proposal has substance, it will help them do their jobs more effectively, and it will not go away.

Improve the Adults

If you're going to make the changes in student learning that account-
ability requires, you have to dramatically increase the skill and knowl-
edge of teachers and principals.

Dr. Richard Elmore,
Harvard University

I believe that at-risk students have a hard time seeing themselves as successful and as a result work to please others. It is therefore especially important for teachers to relate to the at-risk student.

Sheila Newkirk-Squire, Buerhle Alternative School

School improvement, and everything that surrounds and sometimes shrouds the subject, comes down to one simple process: improving the mindset and performance of the adults. The children will reap the rewards, in direct proportion to the quality and efficacy of the professional development. Simply put, when a leader can improve the work of the adults in the school building, the children come along for the ride.

The No Child Left Behind world attaches far too much importance to subject-matter knowledge and technical proficiency. When adults are asked to describe the best teacher they had in school, most tell about someone who made them feel valued or special. Very rarely do they speak of a teacher's technical excellence. Yes, subject-matter knowledge is extremely important, but the only way to build a school that meets the needs of all students is to staff it with people who actually care for children.

> In interviews with dropouts, the best teachers were seen as caring
> individuals who tried to give extra help when students struggled.
> In contrast, the poorest teachers were seen as being uncaring and
> the worst were described as mean. This research clearly indicates
> that improving the school, from a student perspective, is as "easy"
> as developing a more caring faculty. (Morris, 1994)

In part because they *get* the premise of the preceding passage, several principals we surveyed report gearing the entire interview process toward determining whether a candidate actually likes young people. Leaders can teach teachers how to teach. They cannot teach teachers to love children. A teacher who does not love children has no place in a classroom.

No principal can expect to dramatically change the quality of the children who come through the school doors. After all, parents aren't sending their worst children to school and keeping the best ones at home. Far too many school leaders and teachers focus professional development on fixing the students—trying to change things that may not ever change, rather than preparing adults to meet and overcome the challenges at hand. This creates frustration for the adults without making a difference to the students.

Some might say, "This is the way school is done. It has worked in the past, it should be good enough for today's students." Or "Where is the responsibility?" We do not suggest for a minute that schools shouldn't hold students accountable for their actions. But often the habits of at-risk students do not fit the mold of traditional *schooling*. We waste far too much energy trying to get everyone to fit that mold, and far too many students drop out along the way. One-size-fits-all education never worked. Educators who want to make a difference to the at-risk student must find a more creative approach.

> Our key to success is that students perceive our school to be positive and integral to their future success.
>
> *Richard Storm*, Union Alternative School

Although it may seem simplistic, the key to addressing the needs of all at-risk students is to ensure that they see a need for what is asked of them. Granted, that is not as easy as it sounds; but it becomes a much more doable task when schools start to strip away all the pretenses that surround the educational process and look at exactly what they are doing and why they are doing it. Anything that does not enhance the students' perception of the school as positive and integral to their success detracts from that perception. There is no middle ground. Several schools highlighted in this book initiated their school improvement plan by simply looking at all their processes and determining whether each one added to the school's quality and student performance or diminished it. Many described the approach as cathartic because it forced the adults in the school to look inward for answers as opposed to blaming children.

> We moved from being a school that was about maintaining the status quo and comfort for teachers to one that is more child centered and focused on continuous improvement.
>
> *Linda Welch*, Whittier School

> We have moved from the attitude, "They're different or broken—you fix them." to "What can we all do to help this child succeed?"
>
> *Pat Sievers and Julie Stoneburner*, Ankeny Community School District

These schools have managed to succeed where many others with similar demographics have not. Although their methods may have varied, they all ended up with schools that address the needs of all children because the adults continually adapt to address those needs. Such environments generally validate the worth of a child; and as several principals said in one way or another, a validated and valued child most often becomes a motivated learner.

Traditionally, schools have operated on the premise that children must adapt to them, not the other way around. But that paradigm was responsible for the downfall of the American auto industry when it resisted adapting to consumers' preference for Japanese imports. It led to the crippling of IBM when it was slow to move from a mainframe-computer–centered business model and embrace the rise of the personal computer. It caused the erosion of Kodak's customer base when digital photography decreased the need for film and the cameras that use film. That paradigm has never worked in industry. It has never worked in politics. What unforgivable arrogance to think it will work in our schools.

Professional Development

Professional development is the backbone of school improvement. But schools must build their own long-term programs, focusing on the teaching and learning process and the needs of their own school and students. One-shot, quick-fix, packaged programs do not work. And system reform must focus on improving schools, not on raising test scores or revamping curriculum. Simply *fixing* a single test grade or adding a new science or technology program will not improve student learning. Improved learning should happen across grade levels and between subject areas.

The surest way to improve student achievement is to improve the practice of the adults in the building. If we know this, why do we find it so difficult to accomplish? One answer is the lack of understanding about what makes quality professional development effective. Far too much professional development looks good, sounds good, and may even meet some quality criteria on paper but fails to make a significant difference in adult practice. School systems frequently implement educational initiatives without any evidence that they will work.

More perplexing is the phenomenon that even educators who can rattle off the standards for quality professional development fall short when it comes to implementing them. All too often, we hear school leaders talk about job-embedded, research-based professional development and then invite a guest speaker for a 1-hour seminar at the start of the school year. They may even come right out and say, "We have an hour to fill." Too often, the driving force behind planning is still the schedule of time available, rather than the solid work the data call for.

Many states have adopted a version of the National Staff Development Council (NSDC) Standards as the foundation for designing, delivering and evaluating professional development for educators. Although NSDC published its revised list of 12 professional development standards some five years ago, the quality of professional development continues to vary widely.

For these reasons and many others, we have taken another look at the NSDC Standards as they play out in schools. What do we expect to see in schools that effectively align their practices to the standards? What do we observe in schools that fall short?

National Staff Development Council Standards for Staff Development

Context Standards

Staff development that improves the learning of all students:

- ◆ Organizes adults into learning communities whose goals are aligned with those of the school and district (*learning communities*)
  - *Ineffective:* Leaders link professionals in the building into loosely organized groups or committees and assign them tasks not directly related to improving student achievement. Groups do not develop the protocols necessary to work effectively. Groups usually have general names that sound effective (*school-based building team, learning team, school improvement team*); members may even be able to recite missions and goals, but they rarely see the relationship between their meetings and improvement. The classic example is the grade- or subject-level team that meets regularly but hardly ever looks at student achievement. Usually these teams meet, *talk nice* and produce few results.
  - *Effective:* Leaders place practitioners into working teams with carefully designed protocols, agendas, goals, and responsibilities. They develop layers of responsibility dictated by data-driven needs and involving every member of the professional staff. Teams meet daily, weekly, and monthly. Every meeting focuses on school improvement and involves looking at data, such as student work, unit test results, daily lesson plans, and progress. Faculty meetings routinely address student achievement. Grade-level meetings always center on student unit tests, daily assignment results, homework discussions, and state and local test data.
- ◆ Requires skillful school and district leaders who guide continuous instructional improvement (*Leadership*)

- *Ineffective:* Schools pay lip service to instructional leadership, but leaders don't understand how good instruction looks, sounds, or feels. Many were trained in programs that leaned heavily toward administrative aspects. Those unsure of instructional leadership set up weak structures (such as general improvement teams) but attend meetings rarely, or leave soon after they begin, or lack the self-assurance and know-how to move them forward. Leaders may delegate instructional leadership responsibilities without modeling effective practice. The key word in this standard is *guide.*

- *Effective:* Leaders make data-driven decisions, focus most of their energy on instructional improvement, and understand that they must model strong instruction. They attend grade-level meetings, ensure that faculty meetings are about instruction, and team-teach as often as possible. They set aside protected time every day to visit classrooms, supporting good instruction. Leaders stock their bookcases with current books on instructional improvement and learning. They can speak intelligently about current research on learning styles, special education findings, differentiated instruction, and other instructional strategies and concerns. They ensure that the school celebrates and showcases academic achievement with the same emphasis as other school activities. In short, leaders model day-to-day practices that produce improvement.

- ◆ Requires resources to support adult learning and collaboration (*resources*)

  - *Ineffective:* Leaders call for change without providing necessary resources—funding, time for training, content for training, trainers, and materials. They let budget considerations take priority over needed change.

  - *Effective:* Leaders plan ahead for change, taking into account the resources needed to support it. To maximize the chances for success, they secure resources before embarking on change efforts. When implementing changes in practice, they recognize that training is the most crucial resource; and they ensure funding for training before investing in books, kits, videos, manuals, or other hardware. They make creative and efficient use of in-house expertise.

Process Standards

Staff development that improves the learning of all students:

- ◆ Uses disaggregated student data to determine adult learning priorities, monitor progress, and help sustain continuous improvement (*data-driven*)

  - *Ineffective:* No Child Left Behind has certainly placed the words *disaggregated student data* into the education lexicon. Educators can speak the language of data-driven curricula, decision-making, and improvement. In practice, however, they miss the crucial link between data and adult practice. Educators often jump to what students did not learn or what students should do differently. Leaders focus on curriculum change without addressing the need to improve pedagogy. Teachers stop short of understanding that the problem may be in their practice rather in the curriculum, in time spent teaching, or in student capabilities.

  - *Effective:* Leaders analyze the full range of factors that influence student achievement, giving top priority to the teaching practices of adults in the building. Teachers look first at improving their practice, and only then move to the curriculum, time on tasks, student weaknesses, and other concerns. Educators learn to target weaknesses in their practice, spread the lessons learned, and continue developing the skills of teaching. Once they are sure that they are doing no harm, educators explore the other reasons students may not be progressing at desired levels.

- ◆ Uses multiple sources of information to guide improvement and demonstrate its impact (*evaluation*)

  - *Ineffective:* Schools look only at the results of state-mandated tests, usually after students have moved to another grade level, rather than using benchmarks multiple times during the year to measure progress. Intensive use of benchmarks early in the year too often dwindles as other challenges take priority. Grade-level meetings do not regularly and systematically review students' grasp of key concepts before the summative test. Leaders also often fail to take advantage of all the available sources that can give information about their schools.

    Victoria Bernhardt (1998) emphasizes four areas of data that leaders should take into consideration when working to improve schools. She points out that in two areas (student achievement data and demographic data), educators have learned to gather a great deal of information. However, in the other two (school processes and perceptions of others about the school), we hardly scratch the surface. It has been our experience in training educators that few even understand the concept of school processes: the day-to-day functions of the school. We highly recommend Bernhardt's book.

- *Effective:* School leaders understand that discipline, interruptions, celebrations, paperwork, and other necessary processes can affect instruction. They collect data about these processes to make decisions that support teaching and learning. They also know that stakeholders' beliefs about the school can make a difference to teaching and learning, among other things. They make perceptions from those inside and outside the building an important part of the yearly data-gathering practice.

◆ Prepares educators to apply research to decision making (*research based*)

- *Ineffective:* Principals often do not know how to help staff apply what they learn from data sources to the decisions they must make. They overlook the relationship between discipline processes that remove students from the classroom and the negative impact on their achievement. They miss the possible connection between test results showing low scores across a grade level and poor pedagogy, poor student attendance, or worse, poor teacher attendance. They regard *research based* as the domain of scholars who write books about theories and present data to support their conclusions. Underestimating the relevance of data gathered by teachers, parents, students, and others in the school environment, they look to outside research to support their decisions.

- *Effective:* Leaders base decisions on data derived from careful analysis of processes, learning, teaching, perceptions, demographics, and scholarly works. Decisions and solutions emerge from relevant facts. Leaders draw on a range of published works to support decisions, but they also value action research led by teachers in the building. Leaders and professional staff have confidence in their ability to research a problem and base decisions on their findings. Decisions about teaching and learning are made not because they feel right but because the research done inside or outside the school points to the decision.

- ◆ Uses learning strategies appropriate to the intended goal (*design*)
  - • *Ineffective:* Armed with a *toolbox* mentality, leaders reach for the program du jour to fix teaching and learning problems. They choose strategies because they look and sound effective or because another school has used them. Often such choices are driven by central office decisions and weakly link strategies to problems uncovered by school data. Leaders rarely give professional staff a voice or choice about which strategy to apply. Inappropriate selection of solutions begets continued failure, low staff morale, and burnout.
  - • *Effective:* Leaders know that there may be many reasons why students are not learning and that there is likely not a panacea. They understand that when professional staff research possible strategies to solve a problem in the same way they researched the data that uncovered the problem, they are more likely to apply the strategies effectively and know when to exercise other options. Leaders promote buy-in from all stakeholders by letting them decide whether the strategy fits the problem. They take a practical approach to school improvement.
- ◆ Applies knowledge about human learning and change (*learning*)
  - • *Ineffective:* Leaders attempt to make improvements by simply proclaiming that change will happen. They do not understand their role in modeling the change or are unwilling to change their own practice first. They often express bewilderment that they are leading and no one is following. Steeped in their study of how children learn, they imagine they can lead their professional staff in similar ways. They underestimate the complexity of adult learning and the human reaction to change.
  - • *Effective:* Leaders appreciate the complexity of adult learning. They understand that what motivates adults to learn is very different from what motivates children, that change is more difficult the older one gets, and that simply demanding change is not likely to work. Knowing that real change in schools starts with adult practice, leaders empower those who own the practice to drive the change. They expect adults to be self-directed, use their life experiences, and see relevancy in what they must learn. Leaders build a case for change, giving the professional staff autonomy to work through its stages and

to scaffold small changes on small changes to attain the goal of complex reform.

- ◆ Provides educators with the knowledge and skills to collaborate (*collaboration*)
  - *Ineffective:* Leaders assign staff to committees, work with the PTA on a project or two during the year, and that's it. They have little experience of team teaching, group problem solving, cross-curricular work, grade-level meetings, interdisciplinary teaching, and other such tactics. The egg-crate philosophy of school prevails: all teachers in their rooms, doors closed, and as much silence as possible. Math teachers have their niche, English teachers have theirs—no omelets please! Teachers buy into the status quo because true collaboration is sometimes painful and always time-consuming. They cling to the autonomy they enjoy behind closed doors, view interaction with other professionals as a threat, and push back when the leader suggests collaboration.
  - *Effective:* Knowing that collaboration flourishes only when adults understand the reason for it and can see dividends for the time spent, leaders take time to develop the necessary knowledge and skills. They start with small, more comfortable opportunities for interaction, building a history of success to underpin complex efforts that have high-stakes results. Leaders value informal collaboration, such as two teachers standing in the hall discussing what they might do to reach Johnny, and provide training to maximize its efficacy.

Content Standards

Staff development that improves the learning of all students:

- ◆ Prepares educators to understand and appreciate all students, create safe, orderly and supportive learning environments, and hold high expectations for their academic achievement (*equity*)
  - *Ineffective:* Students suffer most from ineffective practice here. Leaders who blame poor student achievement on student demographics simply remove responsibility from those who must find a way for every student to learn. Of particular concern is the practice of supporting some students for certain achievements, often athletics, but giving only lip service to academic achievement and excellence in the arts. Leaders may

set high expectations for students and faculty without providing the leadership for achievement.

- *Effective:* Leaders make this standard their number one priority. They maintain ongoing professional development for staff about inclusion, differences, safety, discipline, and other topics that support a safe and orderly learning environment. Schools celebrate *all* student achievement—the fall musical as much as the Friday night football game. Appreciation of all students, their differences and their achievements, underpins every effort to improve teaching and learning. Discipline issues diminish as students feel valued.

◆ Deepens educators' content knowledge, provides them with research-based instructional strategies to assist students in meeting rigorous academic standards, and prepares them to use various types of classroom assessments appropriately (*quality teaching*)

- *Ineffective:* Leaders perceive teaching as strictly the purview of the classroom teacher and devote most of their own attention to administrative tasks. Teachers take the attitude that when it comes to teaching, principals should be seen and not heard. Leaders settle into the traditional and more comfortable role of *the administrator.* Teachers with weak pedagogy or poor subject-matter knowledge can continue just muddling along. Leaders do not understand, or choose to ignore, their responsibility for improving practice and holding teachers accountable for quality teaching.

- *Effective:* Leaders understand that quality teaching is paramount to improving student achievement and view the principal as the lead teacher. They embrace their role and maximize their influence as instructional leaders. They use their position of responsibility to support better adult practice and to build trust, proving to teachers that they can depend on the principal to support quality teaching with professional development, resources, and good decisions. Leaders hold teachers accountable for knowing their content and for building stronger and stronger pedagogy. Identifying weak practice, they find a way to address the weakness and to provide the support the teacher needs to improve. Coupling accountability with support, they lead improvement, share teaching concerns, and monitor progress.

- ◆ Provides educators with knowledge and skills to involve families and other stakeholders appropriately (*family involvement*)
  - *Ineffective:* Leaders lament the absence of parent support as an insurmountable obstacle to student achievement. They let this excuse stand in the way of efforts to hold students accountable. Leaders—and consequently teachers—find it easier to point the finger at the lack of family involvement than to create momentum for school improvement by focusing on the most important factor for boosting student achievement, namely high-quality teaching.
  - *Effective:* Leaders value parent support, work to build it, and find unique ways to improve it. They research and observe other schools, and there are many nationwide, that have managed to build parent and community involvement or to raise student achievement without it. Leaders remove the excuse of poor parent support from the equation of teaching and learning. They keep the faculty focused on what really counts: what happens in the classroom day in and day out.

Strategic Planning

School districts spend a great deal of time and energy developing strategic plans. Unless and until they deploy these plans, nothing happens. Schools, too, can develop all the strategic plans they wish, but unless they activate their plans, nothing gets done. Too often, educators know *what* to do, but they don't know *how* to implement their plans. All sorts of obstacles—chief among them, a shortage of time, personnel, funding and/or capacity—stand in their way.

Schools that have improved the most have set higher expectations and have offered more support for students and staff to meet these higher standards. They have aligned their plans with those of the local area, state, and federal standards to achieve their objectives. They have then aligned teaching and learning to those standards. Further fine tuning should align classroom content to the goals of the school.

Vision and Mission

Many schools highlighted in this book find themselves in a continual state of flux as they keep metamorphosing to meet the needs of their students. This can be very unsettling without a touchstone—a guide that shows teachers and administrators that they are indeed on the right track.

The first word here may be the most important one: *we*. Effective leaders recognize the need to create ownership of a process to secure staff buy-in. They must do whatever is necessary to ensure that the mission that will drive the school is understood and embraced by the change agents—the faculty.

> We developed a Mission Statement and Educational Philosophy to serve as a touchstone for all decision making.
>
> *Judy Knotts*, St. Gabriel's Catholic School

All successful leaders have a vision and mission. It is the reason they were hired. Although they developed it and they articulate it, other stakeholders—the staff; parents; and frequently, the students—inevitably mold it to fit the needs of the school or district.

A successful mission does the following:

◆ Focuses on learning and student achievement

◆ Is specific to the needs of the school or school district

◆ Is measurable

◆ Is achievable over time

Schools need to develop mission statements that articulate the goals of preparing students to function effectively as the following:

◆ Purposeful thinkers

◆ Effective communicators

◆ Self-directed learners

◆ Productive group participants

◆ Responsible citizens

◆ Workforce-ready employees

◆ Creative problem solvers

◆ Team workers.

Most mission statements are so generic that they are meaningless: "We will have the finest graduates in the world." Too many are not measurable or take growth rates from the sky: "We will improve our reading scores by 100% in the next 2 years." Too often, they need a reality check: "We prepare students for useful lives in the twenty-first century; but few faculty members are computer literate and integrate technology as a natural part of their teaching.

An effective leader must have followers. School leadership is too overwhelming a job for one person to tackle. Good leaders do not impose their goals on followers but work with others to create a shared sense of purpose and direction. Leaders need to create high performance expectations for *all* learners. They help others understand the gap between where the school or district is and where it needs to be. Effective leaders develop and enlist the support of a powerful guiding coalition that understands and endorses the change.

> I facilitated the staff's writing of a school mission and vision statement.
> *Mary Jo McLaughlin*, The Academy of Creative Education

Developing a school's mission and vision must be a group effort—and not just because this increases the probability that all stakeholders will embrace and act on them. Group input usually results in a better product. We found an example of that in the mission and vision statements of Lincoln High School, a small rural high school in Charleston County, South Carolina. The Lincoln High School Mission Statement is as elegant in its simplicity as it is powerful in its intent. The Vision Statement clearly supports the mission. Together, they set the tone for a future in which the school addresses each student's needs. It is important to note that the school struggled to craft a cohesive vision when trying to do so in separate committees. However, the mission, vision, and supporting beliefs statements were developed and agreed on in an extended and honest conversation that took place during a schoolwide summer retreat. Significantly, when they were done, the faculty and staff agreed that *their* work would make their school better.

Mission Statement

The mission of Lincoln High School is to provide a high-quality education for each student.

Vision Statement

We envision Lincoln High School as being an example of notable excellence in achievement. We see our students as 'superstars'—highly motivated and having a wealth of opportunities. We envision the faculty, staff, administration, students, home, and community actively working together respectfully and cooperatively as a unified force to accomplish our mission and to make our vision a reality.

Beliefs

We believe:

- All students can learn.
- Students learn best in a safe, orderly, and nurturing environment.
- A high-quality education prepares students to succeed in an ever-changing world.
- A high-quality education builds character and promotes critical thinking, decision-making, problem solving, personal accountability, and effective communication.
- A high-quality education develops leadership in students.
- The faculty and staff of Lincoln High School are responsible for ensuring a high-quality education for each student.
- Students must be active participants in the learning process.
- Lincoln High School requires the support and input of the home and surrounding community to be successful in providing a high-quality education.

In *Failing Is Not an Option,* Alan Blankstein (2004) offers six principles that guide student achievement in high-performing schools:

1. Common mission, vision, values, and goals
2. Systems for prevention and intervention
3. Collaborative teaming for teaching and learning
4. Data-driven decision-making and continuous improvement
5. Active engagement from family and community
6. Building sustainable leadership capacity

These six principles support the need for a comprehensive and shared mission, vision, and beliefs. Furthermore, they attest to the importance of structures that legitimize the beliefs. If a school purports to believe that *all students can learn,* it must provide a foundation of structures to flesh out that belief. Strategies such as mentoring programs, differentiated instruction, learning contracts, after-school remediation, tiered lesson plans, and others like them put the belief that *all students can learn* into concrete practice. Otherwise, the statements are just words on a page.

Chapter Summary

The key to school improvement is to improve the mindset and performance of adults within the school. Meaningful change demands careful planning, coordination, collaboration, and understanding. Leaders embarking on school improvement must prepare to encounter resistance. To build effective professional development programs, schools must focus on the teaching and learning process and the needs of their own school and students. Developing a school's mission and vision must be a group effort.

The answers to two simple questions can help any leader determine how gravely improvement is needed:

1. Does the intrinsic motivation of your students increase the longer they attend your school?

2. Does the intrinsic motivation of your teachers increase the longer they work at in your school?

6

Staff Empowerment

The fundamental concept in social science is power, in the same sense in which energy is the fundamental concept in physics.

Bertrand Russell

Schools across the nation share many similarities in their knowledge base. The difference in their performance largely depends on their school's leaders' ability to energize and activate that base. A principal cannot, nor ever could, effectively address the needs of at-risk students. Only a faculty can do that. The effective leader must find ways to tap the skills and resources, the power, of every teacher. School improvement begins with adult improvement; but adult improvement begins when teachers view themselves as owners, not merely occupants, of the school.

> Our school really started to improve when we upgraded the process for shared decision-making—more opportunities had to be established for teachers to step forward as teacher leaders.
>
> *Linda Maxwell*, Oak Mountain Intermediate School

> I started by building trusting relationships between myself and the teachers, constantly complimenting their good points and letting them know that I valued their hard work. I observed them a lot and always found something to praise. They began to realize that I really liked and admired them and that I trusted their judgment with kids.
>
> *LaVeral Graf*, W. C. Griggs Elementary School

The principals highlighted in this book realize that their relationship with staff and faculty has a major impact on their students. At the risk of oversimplifying a complex matter, they understand that a disgruntled staff makes for an unsettled student body and that unsettled adolescents slide into at-risk learners. Although these school leaders set very high standards for their teachers, they are manifestly human in their dealings with them. Each is keenly aware that leadership is impossible unless there is someone willing to follow. They work to build relationships so that leadership is possible.

Trust is the lubricant that allows organizations to run smoothly. One of its primary byproducts is open and honest communication. That communication engenders an environment where faculty and staff feel able to take risks to reach children. Only educational risk taking, on the part of both teachers and students, opens the door to breakthroughs in achievement. A popular definition of insanity is "doing the same thing over and over again the same way and expecting a different outcome." Unfortunately, that happens in many schools across our nation, because leaders have not built an environment that invites and supports change. Unless a faculty is freed from the shackles of self-doubt by a leader who trusts and supports them, true innovation is improbable, if not impossible.

People rarely develop trust at a distance. Great teachers do not teach from the front of the classroom; they teach in the midst of the learners. Likewise, great leaders cannot distance themselves from the faculty and staff; they must lead from within, building relationships and earning trust. The key to success is effective communication that permits a constant flow of information from top to bottom and from bottom to top.

> I gently push them into taking risks. They know I respect them and their professionalism.
>
> *Pat Sievers and Julie Stoneburner,* Ankeny Community School District

Listen to Each Other

In the traditional model of school, how often were teachers asked for their professional opinions? How often were they treated like hired hands, given a list of tasks and duties, expected to simply follow orders? How often did principals or superintendents overlook their faculty's education and experience? How often did schools squander their most valuable resource?

> We have staff meetings devoted to discussing problems, brainstorming solutions, sharing ideas, and otherwise developing ties of interdependency. We enjoy our time together.
>
> *Richard Storm,* Union Alternative School

> Most of my successful strategies have involved the development of teams. I encourage the staff to provide "honest feedback" in their work with each other and try to model it myself.
>
> *Cliff Downey,* Mooroopn Park Primary School

> I adjust my communication style to accommodate others as necessary.
>
> *Larry Sholes,* Attucks Alternative Academy

In a recent workshop presented to a large group of principals and teacher leaders in Birmingham, Alabama, the panel asked, "Are you the smartest, most knowledgeable person in your school?" Not a single principal answered in the affirmative. The follow-up question was, "Then why do you so often hesitate to ask the people who frequently have the most knowledge—your teachers—for help in making decisions?" No principal can do it alone; every principal lacks knowledge in some areas—and the odds are that at least one teacher can fill the gap. Effective leaders make abundant use of their staff's knowledge and expertise.

Teachers see the big picture. They can discern what students can achieve. They are on the front line day after day. They know what works and what doesn't. Give them room for flexibility, and they can make immediate adjustments. Ask them to evaluate curriculum, syllabi and textbooks, and they can maximize the worth of every hour and every dollar. Invite them to the roundtable, and strategic plans become solid blueprints and then effective programs. No school leader can afford to ignore their valuable contributions.

Effective communication can invigorate a faculty. However, that communication must take many forms. John Wooden, one of the greatest coaches and communicators of all time, was once asked why he treated Bill Walton differently from his other players. The reporter said it appeared that Wooden had a double standard. Wooden replied that he had 12 players, so he had 12 standards. Certainly everyone must meet minimum standards, but treating people as individuals maximizes the probability that they will rise to reach their full potential.

Include the Staff in Making Decisions

> We communicate a vision that includes the need for everyone to be a part of the fix.
>
> *David Basile*, R.B. Stall High School

> The staff has been fully involved in all phases of the development of this program.
>
> *Bruce Smith*, Albuquerque Charter Vocational High School

> We have shared leadership roles. Each year the staff develops team goals and outlines how we will achieve them. We include everyone in the planning, development and implementation of school projects and functions.
>
> *Mary Jo McLaughlin*, The Academy of Creative Education

One common thread woven through the responses highlighted in this book is the commitment to giving staff a voice. The most powerful reason given was that teachers who participate in making decisions are more likely to internalize the outcomes as values. A mission, vision, or belief statement becomes a value only if it is voluntarily chosen. Values drive individuals in ways that directives or orders cannot. Shared values, the kind that arise from collaborative decision making, drive cultures.

Also fairly common among the responses was a second reason, more utilitarian in nature, for including staff and faculty. As the job of principal grows more complex, enlisting the help of others becomes necessary for self-preservation. Numerous principals told us that the input of their faculty eased their burden and raised the quality of the decisions made. They also insisted that the teachers' perspective was essential to decisions about teaching.

Shared leadership makes communication much more honest and open. One principal reported that he finally declared he would no longer accept complaints. He would, however, actively address concerns. He explained that concerns differ from complaints in that concerns are accompanied by prospective solutions. His staff embraced that philosophy, and he soon found that he was frequently offered suggestions for improvements he had never even considered.

Build Collaboration

> Collaboration is the key to stronger ties. We must trust each other and have passionate discussions about student achievement without making it personal. Our teachers are strong, well educated, very opinionated, and dedicated to the success of all students. They are true leaders. We make all decisions together, but they recognize the role of administration.
>
> *Terri Tomlinson*, George Hall Elementary School

Opening up the decision-making process lays the foundation for truly collaborative learning among the staff. Collaborative learning activates and energizes the collective knowledge of any faculty. Although most schools have similar knowledge bases, the successful ones share knowledge, and that sharing of knowledge creates synergy. The principals highlighted in this study shared a strong belief that collaborative faculties are smarter faculties, and that smarter faculties more adequately address the needs of all students.

Principals who leave faculty out of school improvement plans risk failure on all fronts. Teachers represent the largest and most stable group of adults in the school, and their tenure in the school makes them the most politically powerful. The faculty, both collectively and individually, seeks to influence those in key decision-making roles to get things done. Accepting and embracing that fact makes it possible for the principal to focus and control the influence instead of being a slave to it.

Charles Brower once said, "Few people are successful unless a lot of other people want them to be." That is particularly true for principals and superintendents. The criterion for measuring their performance is student achievement, and student achievement depends on the teachers in the classrooms. This simple realization changes the entire context of educational leadership. Principals must guide, evaluate, and counsel but, most importantly, they must support their staff and faculty.

Support Teaching and Learning

To lead a school toward becoming a genuine learning community, the principal must take the role of chief student:

- Conducting and sharing action research
- Participating in limited partnerships
- Showing interest in others' learning
- Creating opportunities for collaborative adult learning
- Modeling lifelong learning

Most classrooms operate in a teacher-driven culture of autonomy and isolation. Most middle and high schools separate colleagues into departments by subject and content. In the typical middle or high school cafeteria, English teachers sit with other English teachers, science teachers with other science teachers, and so on. School floor plans often group classrooms by content area, giving teachers easy access to those who teach a similar subject but infrequent contact with teachers outside their departments. In large schools, teachers in different wings might not even recognize each other in the parking lot. School leaders rarely have the opportunity to dismantle walls and open up corridors, but they should make every effort to build a sense of community among the teachers in their schools.

> We have a book-of-the-month luncheon, regular staff recognition meetings, and sixth-week huddles, which are grade-level planning meetings.
> *Steven Havens, Saltillo Elementary School*

There is a mystique that surrounds teaching. Because teaching is so isolationist and individualistic, teachers believe that they alone control the material taught. The reality is that the content in the classroom has largely been determined by outside forces, including curriculum writers, textbook publishers, and local, state and federal mandates. And, as Steven Barkley of Performance Learning Systems has indicated, there is a major disconnect between teaching and learning (illustrated below).

Teaching Can Be	Learning Often Is
Neat	Messy
Orderly	Spontaneous
Sequential	Irregular
Linear	Nonlinear

Steven G. Barkley, Executive VP, Performance Learning Systems, Southern Regional Education Board Annual Conference, July 13, 2006.

But when school leaders empower teachers to address the needs of all the learners in their classrooms, they open the door to student achievement. Instructional leaders make the most of their faculty's education and experience. Leadership teams with informal leaders or without a formal leadership role have the potential to assist formal leaders. They can help other teachers to embrace goals, understand the changes that are needed to strengthen teaching and learning, and work together toward improvement.

> We have collaborative development of belief statements. We utilize school improvement team members for the delivery of most staff development. We have truly comprehensive input of all team members.
>
> *Linda Welch*, Whittier School

> I give them opportunities to collaborate and move them from one grade if they cannot get along or are more appreciated on another grade level.
>
> *LaVeral Graf*, W. C. Griggs Elementary School

> Grade-level planning and faculty input on decisions that impact students.
>
> *Betty J. Warren*, Huxford Elementary School

Make Classroom Management Matter

Although most educational, political, and business leaders focus on raising educational standards, redesigning curriculum, and monitoring progress through tests, classroom management is still the cornerstone of an effective educational environment. Students must know that learning begins as soon as they walk into the classroom.

Too many entering teachers are not taught the basics of classroom management. Far too many inexperienced teachers feel that they must create a strict set of rules, announce them on the first day of school, and rigidly enforce them with a predetermined set of punishments for any infractions. Others believe that they must serve as a friend to the youngsters in their charge; they fail to provide the structure that a classroom needs. The answer to classroom control probably lies somewhere in the middle; teachers who want to influence the behavior of most young people must achieve some sort of balance between being too strict and too friendly.

Novice teachers frequently get the worst schedules, in the lowest-performing schools—without mentoring, supervision, or adequate administrative support. Many start with the impression that asking for assistance is a sign of weakness, and many schools do nothing to change that impression. Many potentially effective teachers quit in despair because they cannot get their classrooms under control. Data show that 46% of teachers leave the system and teaching within five years. The system eats its young.

Although schools of education have been focusing on increased standards and knowledge of pedagogy and subject matter, they find it difficult to teach potential educators how to control a classroom because the candidates lack a contextual framework of understanding. But school leaders work with teachers in the context of school. Those who want to meet the needs of all children will focus a good deal of their instructional leadership on the skills of classroom management.

> We provide continual opportunities for dialogue and consistently remind people that there is more than one path to a destination. This work is ongoing due to multiple philosophical perspectives on learning and the presence of "old wounds."
>
> *Mark Linton*, Geneseo Elementary School

Many school leaders see no connection between instructional leadership and the administrative aspects of their jobs. They often talk about the two sets of tasks competing for their time and attention. Effective leaders do not abandon management or disciplinary responsibilities, but they do consider how their actions in those areas can best contribute to student learning.

Instructional leaders know that the wrong kind of disciplinary decision can undermine student learning. Milli Pierce, the director of the Harvard Principal Center for 20 years, tells this story: As a classroom teacher, she went to the office each day during her planning period to check her mailbox. Every day, she found young men sitting on the floor, backs against the wall, just waiting. Day by day, the number seemed to grow; soon she had to step over them to get to her mailbox. Finally, she could stand it no more. When she asked the principal why these students sat there, he replied that Mrs. X could not manage them. This was his way of keeping the peace. Concerned for the students' learning, Milli asked to have the young men come to her room each day. For the rest of the year, she used her planning period to teach the students her colleague found unteachable.

Classroom management paves the way for student achievement. Effective educators know how to put the energy in a classroom to work.

Protect the Principal's Golden Hour

The best-laid plans of educators go awry because *school happens*. All school leaders have made great daily agendas, only to find few if any tasks checked off at the end of the day. Schools are such dynamic institutions that they seem to have lives of their own, engulfing leaders in urgent but time-consuming tasks.

Successful instructional leaders take charge of their day. With support from the superintendent, they announce to parents, faculty, and other stakeholders that they set aside 1 hour a day for working on instructional improvement. This can make all the difference in a school; 1 hour per day, 5 hours per week, of concentrated work on instruction can send a powerful message.

The hour must become such a part of the daily routine that it would take a pretty serious set of circumstances to prevent the principal from visiting classrooms, working with a novice teacher, leading a book study, or accomplishing some other instructional support task. Believe it or not, principals who have tried this simple plan find that the school does not fall apart if they routinely leave the office at the same time each day to work with teachers on instruction. Effective leaders respect the skills of their staff; they know how to delegate responsibility. The school secretary can usually keep things rolling as well as, if not better than, most principals.

Maximize the Teacher's Day

> Hosting faculty-run meetings. We have a faculty/staff led "Funs Committee." We also emphasize that sharing and not hoarding knowledge and skills is what we expect in our school.
>
> *Judy Knotts*, St. Gabriel's Catholic School

> Create opportunities for the teachers to work and learn together. We have an active Teacher Leadership Team.
>
> *Linda Maxwell*, Oak Mountain Intermediate School

> Providing the best professional development available. Grade-level and cross–grade-level meetings.
>
> *Deborah Lazio*, Chester Dewey School #14

We also need to restructure a teacher's workday. Many people believe that the only time teachers are working is when they are in front of a classroom. But teachers need time to plan, to reflect, and to talk with their colleagues about teaching methods, problems, and the needs of individual students. We expect doctors and other professionals to keep up with the latest research in their fields; we should provide ample opportunities for educators (including principals and superintendents) to do the same. Professional development, like instructional leadership, deserves *quality time.*

In the olden days, teachers seldom visited one another's classroom or held conversations about curriculum. Schools have increasingly recognized the need for collaboration. But before school leaders start asking for collaboration as part of the daily routine, they must also recognize that collaboration shouldn't happen for its own sake. It must be immediately useful.

Dos and Don'ts for Professional Development

Don't   Plan professional development to fill a time slot.

Do   Plan professional development to fill an identified need for improving practice to raise student achievement.

Don't   Hold a faculty meeting for any reason other than instructional improvement.

Do   Use faculty meetings primarily for professional development for the instructional staff. Restrict any information or tasks that do not touch on student learning to no more than 10 minutes.

Don't   Ask teachers to come early (when they have the day's work on their minds) or stay later (when they are tired and have other responsibilities) to learn the latest new technique or strategy to *make their jobs easier.*

Do   Structure professional development into the regular workday.

Don't   Hold a faculty meeting in an auditorium or media center.

Do   Hold faculty meetings in classrooms. Plan a semester calendar that details when the faculty will meet in which classroom. Announce that at the beginning of the meeting, the hosting teacher will be responsible for sharing an instructional strategy that will work across the curriculum. If the faculty is too large to meet in one classroom, plan departmental meetings. With this plan, teachers are more likely to clean their rooms, renew their bulletin boards, and keep current student work on display.

Practice What You Preach

A school's culture—the fabric that holds the school together—is hard to define, but we know it when we see it. The school culture shows up in statements like these:

◆ This is how we do things around here.

◆ We don't allow that here.

◆ We expect _____ to do this or that.

◆ Our norms are _____.

◆ Our goals are _____.

◆ We believe that _____.

Often, behind these statements lie unspoken but very powerful messages that too many schools continue to wittingly or unwittingly support:

◆ This is how we *say* we do things around here.

◆ We don't allow that here (except for _____).

◆ We expect _____ to do this or that (except these students).

◆ Our norms are _____ (except in the case of_____).

◆ Our goals are _____ (but we probably can't reach them; we haven't figured out the details; and besides, they really aren't *our* goals anyway).

◆ We believe that _____ (unless this problem exists).

Have you ever heard an experienced educator say, "You can fool some of the people some of the time, you can even fool some of the people all of the time, but you can't fool students any of the time"? No truer words were ever spoken. All students, especially the ones at risk, recognize when we talk the talk without walking the walk. Perhaps at no time in education has this truth been more tested than in this era of No Child Left Behind. *All children can learn* has become the mantra of a generation of educators. Too often, our practice makes a very different statement. Let's look at some examples (listed below) of saying one thing and practicing another. As you look at this list, see if you recognize the practices of your school, your colleagues, or maybe yourself.

Belief Statement	Practice
All students can learn.	The most proficient teachers teach only upper-level classes.
Learning is number one.	The intercom interrupts classes all day. Little if any student work is on display. Only athletic trophies are showcased in the lobby.
I am an instructional leader.	There aren't any books concerning teaching or learning in the principal's office. There is never enough time to visit classrooms.
We are a professional learning community.	Faculty meetings rarely address instructional improvement. Bus drivers, custodians, and cafeteria workers are never invited to a faculty meeting and have no stake in student achievement. The faculty has no formal process for visiting colleagues' classrooms.
Grade-level meetings are important.	Student work is never a topic in grade-level meetings.
We value parent involvement.	The only opportunity for parent involvement is a Parent–Teacher Association meeting.

At its core, the culture of any organization is what its leader models and tolerates (Bossidy, Charan, & Burk, 2002). Successful instructional leaders practice what they preach and see to it that their faculties do also. Leaders who make a difference weigh every decision to ensure that the result will be improved student achievement.

> Promote at every opportunity my philosophy of what our school should be—this helps them know what the benchmark is. Keep them apprised of expectations.
> *Karen Petersen*, Northside Alternative Middle School

Power Up the School

Recall the statement that students don't suddenly *drop out* of school in 10th or 11th grade—they *dim out* over time, because school has failed to meet their needs (Schargel, 2005). Students need the energy of a vibrant school culture to keep their lamp of learning from dimming out. Providing that energy, day after day and year after year, requires dedication on the part of all school leaders: the superintendent, principals, teacher leaders, faculty, staff, parents, and community.

12 Behaviors That Underpin a Positive School Culture

1. Genuinely believe that all students can learn and that the school makes the difference between success and failure.

2. Emphasize learning as the most important reason for being in the school, including emphasis on the importance and value of high achievement in their public speeches and writings.

3. Have a clear understanding of the school's mission and be able to state it in direct, concrete terms; establish an instructional focus that unifies the staff.

4. Seek, recruit, and hire staff members who will support the school's mission and contribute to its effectiveness.

5. Know and be able to apply validated teaching and learning principles.

6. Model effective teaching practices for staff as appropriate.

7. Know educational research, emphasizing its importance, sharing it, and fostering its use in problem solving.

8. Seek out innovative curricular programs, observe these, acquaint staff with them, and participate with staff in discussions about adopting or adapting them.

9. Set expectations for curriculum quality through the use of standards and guidelines; periodically check the alignment of curriculum with instruction and assessment, establish curricular priorities, and monitor the implementation of curriculum.

10. Check student progress frequently, rely on explicit performance data, and make results public in addition to using them with staff to find discrepancies between standards and student performance.

11. Expect all staff to meet high instructional standards by securing staff agreement on a schoolwide instructional model, making classroom visits to observe instruction, focusing supervision activities on instructional improvement, and providing and monitoring staff development activities.

12. Communicate the expectation that instructional programs improve over time by providing well-organized, systematic improvement strategies; giving improvement activities high priority and visibility; and monitoring implementation of new practices.

Sandra Lee Gupton (2002)

Encourage Deadwood to Float Away

"If the current is swift and steady, deadwood floats away." When you read this, did you think it referred to students? If so, you missed the point. *Deadwood* refers to the adults in the building who have given up on students.

The illness leading to deadwood adults usually has four stages:

1. Seriously Ill: "I will say all students can learn, but I will not act as though I believe it."

2. On life support: "I am not even going to say all students can learn because I think some of them are destined to fail."

3. Last breath: "I think only some students can learn, and I am not too sure about them."

4. Dead: "Just give me the strength to get to retirement."

At-risk students do not have time for deadwood adults. They need constant support and encouragement. Successful leaders realize that if they can create a current of guided, thoughtful change, the deadwood adults in the building begin to float toward the door. The faster and stronger the current, the more deadwood leave the building. The successful leader creates the current and keeps it strong.

The same current that moves deadwood educators out of a building can empower those who want to support change and improvement. At-risk students should be surrounded by educators who believe students and educators can succeed and understand that achievement takes more time and effort for some students than others. Effective leaders use the power of support and change to create safe harbors in which teachers and students can rest, take stock, and move forward.

In addition, the leader of a school that reaches at-risk students realizes that some students need carefully constructed canals to go from one level of learning to another. Just as the power of water gradually elevates large ships through a series of gated locks, at-risk students need adults who can position them, gradually raise the tasks and expectations around them, and then lift them to a new level of learning.

Chapter Summary

The surest way to improve schools is to make full use of their most valuable resource—the teachers, the support staff, and the administration. Trust and communication create an environment where faculty and staff feel able to take risks to reach children. Teachers who have a voice in decisions are more likely to internalize the outcomes as values. School leaders should make every effort to build community among their teachers.

Effective classroom management paves the way for student achievement. Instructional leadership and professional development deserve *quality time*. Students need the energy of a vibrant school culture.

7

Parent and Family Involvement

I was blessed with a family that wouldn't let me fall by the wayside even though I would have done it in a heartbeat if I didn't have them.

Colin Powell

The importance of parent and family support in improving student achievement has been well documented. Notice that like Colin Powell, we have enlarged the definition of *parent* to embrace the word *family*. Many of America's children are not raised by their parents. Some live in foster homes or in the custody of aunts, uncles, or grandparents. Some are homeless or raising themselves. Some are even responsible for their parents. This calls for adjustments to the old ways of doing business.

Most of our at-risk learners lack the family support that Colin Powell describes. For many, the only adults they see during their waking hours are those in the educational community. According to the U.S. Department of Education, only 8% of middle school parents are involved as volunteers in school, compared with 33% in the first grade. The department also reports that parents find 52% of interactions with their child's first-grade teachers positive but that drops to only 36% by eighth grade (Shinn, 2002).

Educators know that as a child progresses through the educational system, parental or family involvement wanes. Unfortunately, this happens just at the time when a child is under increased peer pressure to use drugs and alcohol, have sex, commit crimes, or ditch school. Schools where many students are already at risk cannot afford to let this support fall away. If we are to leave no child behind, we must also leave no family behind. We need families to join the push for academic achievement, and we need them to stick with it as their children advance through middle school and high school.

Parents as Partners

Once upon a time, teachers were teachers and parents were parents. Teachers taught children how to read and write, add and subtract, diagram a sentence, and dissect a lab specimen; parents taught practical life skills, values, and beliefs. Roles and responsibilities were clearly defined. As society grew more complex, schools began to take on some of the responsibilities once reserved to the home. Today, parents and teachers share many roles. The boundaries have shifted and blurred. Even the definition of what constitutes a family has changed in America today.

But in the end, both parents and educators want to do what is best for children. The effective schools highlighted in this book value what families have to offer. The successful school leaders we observed take seriously the idea of parents as partners in the learning equation. They know that families have a unique perspective on what children need. They recognize that parents actively engaged in their child's school are more likely to support the school mission and goals. They spend time and resources building partnerships with the adults at home.

School leaders who want to bridge the gap between home and school have shown tremendous creativity, stopping short of outright bribery. Often, the first step is just to get families through the schoolhouse door.

> We have a parent breakfast each month.
> *Steven Havens*, Saltillo Elementary School

> We have social/fun events that both parents and children enjoy.
> *Judy Knotts*, St. Gabriel's Catholic School

Once family members feel comfortable at school, they can contribute in a host of ways. No longer do they simply drop off cookies for the bake sale or cheer from the stands at the basketball game. Today, they monitor hallways and lunchrooms, spruce up for the first day of school, serve on the panel of judges for senior project exhibitions, and add to the ranks of volunteer tutors.

Read to Me, Please!

Bring a volunteer into the reading lab, and anything can happen.

- First graders sounding out the letters of the alphabet hear immediate feedback, one on one.
- Early readers on the brink of tackling *chapter books* on their own will fast-forward into the thick of the plot as the visitor reads the first 10 pages.
- Ninth-graders revising an essay on local history catch their awkward sentences when they read them aloud to someone else.
- Students learning English have a chance to practice saying, "rough, through, bough, although" and relieve the tension by laughing about so many different ways to pronounce the same four letters!
- Math students learn to translate word problems into simple equations: *is* means =, *and* means +, *what* gets written down as X or Y. Half an hour of practice goes by quickly when a tutor patiently offers support.

The more parents we can draw into our schools, and the more widely we can engage their talents and interests, the stronger we become.

> Our parent liaisons are very active in school committees.
> *Linda Maxwell*, Oak Mountain Intermediate School

Effective school leaders make a deliberate effort to develop a close working relationship among staff, students, parents and community organizations. One way to build that relationship is to develop written contracts between the school and the home. Expectations outlined in the contract might include the following for parents:

> We have parents who help make decisions for our uniforms—and for our School Action Plan for Excellence.
>
> *LaVeral Graf*, W.C. Griggs Elementary School

- ◆ Attend parent meetings and participate in at least one committee
- ◆ Volunteer at the school on a regular basis.
- ◆ Participate in the decision- making process about school policies, curriculum, and budgets.

On the school's part, the expectations may be as follows:

- ◆ Get to know family members by name.
- ◆ Report absences and tardiness promptly.
- ◆ Maintain regular communication about academic progress.

Such contracts would go a long way toward eliminating misconceptions about the need for parental involvement, while simultaneously emphasizing the school's sincerity about welcoming parents as part of the schooling process.

Communicate, Communicate, Communicate

> We provide newsletters and fliers in both English and Spanish. Active PTA, 21st Century/Extended Day program helps with families where both parents work.
>
> *Bill Aaron*, Asbury High School

> We publish newsletters; conduct parent workshops and mentoring groups. We pair with the Chamber of Commerce as an Education Task Force, which provides a great network for everyone
>
> *Pat Sievers and Julie Stoneburner*, Ankeny Community School District.

> Not only do we invite parents into our school, but also we have hired a parent advocate to make the process easier for them.
>
> *David Besile*, R. B. Stall High School

The first step in welcoming parents and families is to keep them informed of what goes on in the school and the district. Schools must reach out by whatever means are available. Newsletters, flyers posted in local businesses, e-mails sent to the home and employers, or announcements in churches and community organizations about impending open houses and meetings and school websites can increase family participation. Schools also must make parent meetings and family events interesting, relevant, engaging, and positive.

Effective schools keep up a steady flow of feedback to parents, and not just when trouble rears its head. Counselors and other support personnel should make affirmative phone calls thanking parents for sending their children on time, prepared to work with appropriate tools like paper, pens, and other instructional materials.

One principal of an alternative school reported using upbeat phone calls to great effect. Whenever he heard about or saw a student doing something good or scoring well on a test when that was not the norm, he would call the student's parents. He always ended the conversation by saying, "I am very proud of your child, and I knew you would want an opportunity to say how proud you are, too." He would then hand the phone to the student so the parent and the child could have a positive conversation. The principal asserted that the phone calls changed the entire tenor of the relationship between the parents and the school. He also credits the calls with making families more willing to participate in school-sponsored activities.

Counselors should monitor the academic performance of at-risk learners, with immediate feedback to both parents and students if students fall short of mastering the material taught. Waiting until the end of a marking period or term to notify parents that their child has failed a subject puts parents in a position where they cannot do anything about the situation. That is akin to handing them an autopsy report; no matter how detailed and accurate, it is worth far less than an early diagnosis.

Schools also must make it possible for parents to monitor their child's academic progress. They can do so though the use of e-mails, hotlines, even websites where teachers can post assignments on a weekly basis. Keeping parents informed goes a long way toward keeping students on the path to achievement.

> We write a Parent Bulletin every Monday and have a website for parents to go to for homework and news about the school.
>
> *LaVeral Graf*, W. C. Griggs Elementary School

If a child has had a disruptive incident in a classroom or the school, school personnel should meet with the parent to develop a strategy to avoid recurrence and provide assistance if outside referral is advisable. Schools must keep family adults informed of school rules, alternative programs, grades, absences and disciplinary actions. Otherwise, part of the blame for a troubled situation sits squarely on the shoulders of the school and its leaders.

Homework: More Harm Than Good?

Schools must be acutely aware of the repercussions of their homework policies, particularly for at-risk students and their families. Consider this scenario: A student who can barely keep up with the pace of algebra class takes home a sheet of binomial multiplication problems and gets stuck on the second one. Can we automatically expect that an adult at home remembers "FOIL: first—outer—inner—last" and how to apply it? Do you? Or consider the biology student trying to decipher the parts of a cell. Can we assume that someone at home can help? Can we even assume that the at-risk student has time to work on the problem, or a quiet place to do so?

If not, assigning homework is a callous decision that borders on the absurd. Such decisions often lead to frustration in the home that evolves into ill feelings toward the school. The outcome is rarely positive for either the student or the school. Schools that truly care about the welfare of their at-risk students must address their homework policy or run the risk of both losing students and alienating their families.

Educators may not be able to change the fact that Johnny comes to school without his homework. They often find it difficult to change the fact that Johnny's parent won't consistently support the school's efforts to have Johnny do his homework. Rather than spending professional development and planning time on ways to get Johnny to bring his homework, educators should devote time and energy to learning about homework, its effective use, its design, its impact on student learning, and alternative ways to practice new concepts or to get feedback from students about their learning. *Classroom Instruction That Works* does a great job of explaining homework and presenting research data about its effective use for various grade levels (Marzano, Pickering, & Pollock, 2001).

Buttresses and Bridges

Schools that strive to meet the needs of all learners cannot stop at strengthening their own programs. The bridge that effective educators build between school and home is a two-way street. It brings parents and family members into the school, and it sends the lessons and messages of school home with students every day.

Many parents of struggling students did not have positive experiences in schools themselves. They may think of the schooling process as inherently unfair. They may not value an education system that they perceive did not value them. They may not offer the support their children need. But if we can prove to them that we value them as parents, we may win them over. If we can build a relationship with them through continual, honest communication, we may strengthen the environment for learning at home as well as at school. Consider the image of a sturdy bridge, buttressed securely at both ends. That is the learning environment we seek for students at risk.

Chapter Summary

Parent and family support contributes significantly to improving student achievement. Effective schools keep up a steady flow of communication with parents. Parents actively engaged in their child's school are more likely to support the school mission and goals. Effective school leaders make a purposeful effort to build bridges between school and family, especially families of at-risk students.

8

School–Community Collaboration

I not only use all the brains that I have, but all that I can borrow.

Woodrow Wilson

Schools are an integral part of the community. It is the local community that sends its children to school; it is the residents of the community who pay for and benefit from schools. After all, excellent schools draw businesses to the area and stimulate the economy.

In this increasingly complex, industrialized world and information age, schools cannot do the job of educating on their own. Business and community organizations should assume a supportive role with regard to the school, including the donation of financial and in-kind resources.

But it goes beyond that. Businesses should not be perceived as *bottomless pockets* to absorb the costs that the community doesn't fund. Schools have a tendency to ask for increased inputs (more teachers, more classrooms, more technology, more money), whereas the community wants greater outputs (higher graduation rates, lower dropout rates, more students being prepared for college, greater accountability). School leaders must respect the community's desire for the schools to add value to the community.

Parents and business leaders are upset about schools that do not meet the needs of the students. They show their concern by asking for alternatives to public schools in the form of magnet schools, charter schools, alternative schools, or home schooling. To address this dissatisfaction, public school leaders should show the community a return on its investment by proactively reaching out to the community through a public relations plan and a business plan stipulating what the schools need and what the community will get in return.

An effective school–community plan must be systematic, comprehensive, achievable, and ongoing. Good school–community practices can enhance the public's perception of the school. Several state legislatures have enacted legislation that requires community input into school decision making. Effective school leaders know firsthand not only what is going on in their schools or districts but what is happening in the community as well.

Our nation is aging at a rapid rate. In the next 25 years, 27 states will have more than 20 percent of their population over 65. Most seniors have no daily contact with adolescents. Only one household in four has a child of public school age....Principals can play a vital role in ensuring that senior citizens see the school as a vital asset. (Hodkinson, 2000)

The purpose of school–community collaboration is to directly improve and enhance learning opportunities for students, thereby boosting their achievement. This effort requires a process of increasing understanding between the schools and its communities. Leaders who open lines of communication built on mutual respect encourage a win–win situation (Pawlas, 2005). Effective leaders find ways to involve the community in student learning.

In *The Administrator's Guide to School–Community Relations,* George E. Pawlas (2005) lists the 10 components of a well-developed school–community relations plan:

1. Provide the people with information about their schools.
2. Provide the school with information about the community.
3. Establish and maintain public confidence in the schools.
4. Secure community support for the school and its program.
5. Develop a commonality of purpose, effort, and achievement.
6. Develop in the community recognition of the vital importance of education in our social and economic life.
7. Keep the community informed of new trends and developments in education.
8. Develop an atmosphere of cooperation between the school and other social institutions of the community.
9. Secure an evaluation of the school's program in terms of educational needs as the community sees them.
10. Develop public goodwill toward the school.

Although most school–community plans share similarities, no one-size-fits-all plan can ensure success. Certainly, communities have some common characteristics, but Pawlas identifies six factors that make communities differ from one another:

1. Tradition and cultural background
2. Sets of values the community holds
3. Economic bases
4. Geographic features
5. Social structure
6. Political structure

It would be difficult to find two communities that match in all six factors. Therefore, schools must adapt the content and focus of their plans to address the realities of the communities they serve.

Hodkinson's (2000) revelation that only one in four U.S. households has a child of public school age underscores the need for schools to reach out to communities. Otherwise, they must rely on media goodwill to paint a positive picture of public education, not an effective strategy to date. The need to actively recruit community support intensifies in districts serving the poor. The perception prevails in many areas, especially poor neighborhoods, that schools are insular and care little about the surrounding community. In many other communities around the nation, people feel that public education has failed them; they dismiss public school teachers as individuals with little intelligence and even less motivation.

The schools highlighted in this book recognize that strong school–community relationships matter for more than financial reasons, for more than changing attitudes or perceptions. Only through developing strong school–community relationships can a school thoroughly understand the students it serves. Children arrive at school with a view of society that has its roots in their home life and surroundings. That socially constructed reality permeates everything they see and do. A school that presupposes it can meet the needs of all students without a basic understanding of where those students come from has set itself up for failure. The schools that contributed to this book acknowledge the need for community involvement, and they act on it.

Many school leaders mistake sporadic cooperation or intermittent involvement for community collaboration. The well-meaning, short-term partnerships that many school systems have developed over recent years certainly fill a need. However, authentic school–community collaboration goes much farther than that. We define authentic school–community collaboration as the day-to-day presence of community elements working with schools and the school district to support student learning. Authentic collaboration calls for real, long-term commitments on the part of the community and the school in every aspect of the work at hand.

Leaders who develop authentic community collaboration for their schools have parents, grandparents, business people, supporters of the arts, city and county policymakers, and others serving on school committees, working in classrooms, reading to students, lecturing on their specialties, or guiding the faculty through a process that might be foreign to educators. They also have working relationships with museums, fire stations, police departments, hospitals, nonprofit organizations, churches, and other organizations.

Successful school leaders find ways to include community members on as many decision-making panels, boards, committees, and planning councils as possible. Effective leaders create advisory groups of school and community partners to ensure cultural experiences for students or to plan other creative learning experiences. Commitments are real and carefully planned. Authentic collaboration involves community members in grant writing, in problem solving, and in decisions that make a difference because they are important decisions.

Authentic Collaboration:
A Testament to Effectiveness

Authentic collaboration can lead to amazing results. A comprehensive school with grades K through 12 wanted to create a more hands-on approach to learning for their students, especially in social studies. The faculty felt that students were not grasping many of the concepts taught in the social studies curriculum. Teacher-made tests yielded data that indicated poor student achievement. The Advanced Placement (AP) test scores for the older students also showed that social studies students were not getting the foundation they needed in the early grades. The AP Social Studies test scores ranked lowest in the school's AP score portfolio.

The faculty looked at packaged programs and strategies offered for sale by various vendors. Nothing seemed right. About this time, the principal of the school was serving on a civic club task force that brought various professionals together to look at community problems and brainstorm for possible solutions. As he sat in a task force meeting, it dawned on him that this model might offer a way to resolve the social studies problem. The principal shared his idea with the social studies faculty and then with the entire staff. A social studies improvement committee was formed.

At first, the approach was to bring in parents and grandparents who might have some background in social studies or related subjects. After looking at the school social studies curriculum and talking with the staff about teaching approaches, the committee zeroed in on the need for artifacts and hands-on activities for all students. Quickly, the social studies improvement committee grew to include a member of the local historical society, an assistant museum curator, and a local antique dealer. Almost as quickly, the idea emerged to create a history lab filled with historical artifacts to support student inquiry and experiential learning.

The committee began to think of where the school might house a social studies lab. The principal offered to clean out a storage space once used for textbooks that now only held supplies. The history lab became a reality when parents, grandparents, and other stakeholders were asked to donate artifacts that might be used to teach students about the past. The faculty determined a list of items for each grade level and each subject. Before long, the space filled with churns, arrowheads, memorabilia from World Wars I and II, political buttons, an icebox, and even a 1953 RCA Victor television set complete with roof antenna. Every day, the school received more artifacts that could be used to support the hands-on experiences of social studies students. Authentic collaboration solved a problem, created better instruction, and brought together unusual partners.

This collaboration is authentic because the school brought together community members around a real problem, solved the problem, and continued its relationship with the committee members and others to evaluate the solution and maintain the day-to-day function and support of the history lab. The process of support continued and yielded an outdoor archeological dig and an heirloom garden, all of which the community supports to this day. And, by the way, the school has some of the highest AP Social Studies test scores in the nation.

Authentic collaboration offers more than a casual relationship with a school partner that may or may not continue from year to year. Authentic collaboration creates working partnerships between the school and community around real problems. Authentic collaboration is long term, is problem driven, and results in meaningful support for teaching and learning.

Keep the Conversations Positive

> Everybody loves a winner. I let the community know how their school is doing. We invite community leaders into the school on a regular basis.
>
> *Dale Hancock*, Dutton School

> We have maintained a consistent program of public relations through which the community receives ongoing information about the goals and successes of our program.
>
> *Richard Storm*, Union Alternative School

> We build our community relationship by speaking regularly to community groups, becoming a member of the community steering community, and welcoming community volunteers.
>
> *Cliff Downey*, Mooroopna Park Primary School

A key component of a healthy school–community relationship is good communication. Surprisingly, many schools do not embrace opportunities to communicate; many take it for granted that the community knows what is going on in the school. Schools and school systems cannot influence conversations about the school unless they speak up in those conversations. Unless schools proactively communicate the positives, they will stay stuck on reacting to the negatives. Nobody can win over the neighborhood by hunkering down behind a stone wall.

Administrators work more effectively when they get out of the office and into the thick of school; teachers get better results in the midst of the learners than from the front of the classroom. By the same token, schools work better when they open their doors and actively participate in the community. Such participation makes enlisting the community in efforts to meet the needs of at-risk students much more likely to succeed.

> Administrators belong to community service organizations and work hand in hand to help the community beyond school. We have developed a Quaker Community Partnership.
>
> *Richard Varrati*, New Philadelphia City Schools

Given the critical importance of a healthy school–community relationship, it makes no sense to address that relationship haphazardly. Many schools that contributed to this book have a standing community relations committee whose sole purpose is to disseminate good news about the school and nurture two-way communication. Each school described these committees as a vital link to their overall success. Several schools indicated that the information gleaned from their community relations committees provided the foundation for addressing their students' socially constructed realities. All the schools agreed that they were more able to meet the needs of all children in partnership with the communities from which they come.

Open the School to Community Events

> We have an open invitation to fire and police department members for lunch on campus.
>
> *Priscilla McKnight*, Midland City Elementary School

> We host local basketball games between fire and police departments.
>
> *Lee Mansell*, Foley Intermediate School

More often than not, successful schools function as hubs of the communities they serve. The schools surveyed indicated that their place in the community did not develop by chance. Several schools reported that they actively pursued a community presence in their schools.

In addition, several schools stated that they increase community and parent participation by providing free breakfast to adults who agree to tutor students in reading or math. They noted that the time the volunteers spent in the building opened their eyes to the difficulties and rewards of educating young people. It also showed the students that the entire community was concerned about their education.

Contribute to the Community

> We have developed many new partnerships with surrounding community organizations.
>
> *Deborah Lazio*, Chester Dewey School #14

> We have collaborated with the Local Lions club on several projects.
>
> *Larry Sholes*, Attucks Alternative Academy

> Last year we had our first Activity Day where community volunteers come and share their special talents with our students. This was a special day and was coordinated by staff and our Building Planning Team.
>
> *Mark Linton*, Geneseo Elementary School

These schools use their relationship with their communities to improve the quality of the education they provide their students. However, partnerships with community organizations offer other rewards as well. Many a school's mission or vision includes preparing students to contribute to society. Community partnerships can facilitate education for civic engagement.

Schools describe community service projects as particularly effective methods for building self-esteem in at-risk students. Positive self-esteem, coupled with the increased community spirit and pride that they engender, make community service projects a vital facet of any effort to reach at-risk children.

Chapter Summary

> To prepare students to live as compassionate and caring human beings while enhancing what is taught in the classroom and extending it into the community at large, students engage in community service activities such as working with elementary schools at Optimist Bike Rodeos, participating in city-wide food drives, being buddies with middle school students at the Special Olympics, and adopting families at Christmas.
>
> *Mary Jo McLaughlin*, The Academy of Creative Education

The schools highlighted in this book operate as vital parts of their communities, with authentic collaboration that takes many forms. These schools recognize that strong school–community relationships matter for more than financial reasons or building goodwill. It is only through developing strong school–community relationships that a school learns to understand the socially constructed realities of the students it serves. Reaching out to the community widens the *meaningful learning environment* (Illich, 1970) in which learning occurs best.

9

Prioritization

Set priorities for your goals. A major part of successful living lies in the ability to put first things first. Indeed, the reason most major goals are not achieved is that we spend our time doing second things first.

Robert J. McKain

Much of what happens in schools is unpredictable—a fire in a storage closet, a student falling off a gym apparatus, a fight on the playground, a need for extra substitutes in flu season, a student having a seizure. School leaders develop all sorts of plans, but the unexpected frequently dominates their days. Many school leaders continually "put out fires"—both literally and figuratively. We asked the leaders at the schools we surveyed how they decided what to address first.

It All Starts with Self-Assessment

My first priority was to determine what would impact learning the most with the least amount of change. *Steven Havens*, Saltillo Elementary School

All decisions must lend themselves to a safe and productive environment. *Larry Sholes*, Attucks Alternative Academy

The culture of the school was assessed. Discussion groups were generated to discuss greatest needs with the top three concerns going to the entire faculty. Long- and short-term goals were established. *Linda Maxwell*, Oak Mountain Intermediate School

I addressed the situations that seemed to be 1) harmful to kids and 2) harmful to school climate. The personnel issues were addressed very directly. I have continued to work towards creating a more inclusive environment by using our belief statements as a guide and referring to them frequently. *Linda Welch*, Whittier School

The challenges these leaders faced were as different as the schools themselves. Some of their schools serve students from extremely poor environments, whereas others deal with students who have experienced substantial academic failure, often coupled with disciplinary difficulties. Therefore, we expected to receive a myriad of answers. However, we found a surprising degree of consistency. Most principals we contacted asserted that the first priority of any school should be a commitment to honest self-assessment, both collectively and individually. Honest self-assessment lays the foundation for legitimate improvement. Subsequent priorities varied based on school need, but for most schools, the journey to school improvement began with self-assessment.

The self-assessment performed by the schools highlighted in this book yielded a variety of possibilities for change. In most cases, however, whatever bubbled up during the self-assessment was prioritized based on the impact that it would have on student learning.

Shared Leadership, Stronger Results

> I believe that the faculty and staff know what issues need to be addressed. My role is to create the context in which they can share what they know. I used information that I gathered from interviews and questionnaires to generate a list of items to be addressed. We used a system called "Pareto," voting to prioritize what issues we needed to address.
>
> *Mark Linton*, Geneseo Elementary School

> We took the data from surveys and student testing and used it as the basis for a prioritization process in which all stakeholders had a say.
>
> *David Besile*, R. B. Stall High School

> The staff expressed an overwhelming lack of voice. I needed to provide them with a voice and, in doing so, get them happy in order to ensure a positive impact on students and parents.
>
> *Karen Petersen*, Northside Alternative Middle School

> I solicited suggestions from the faculty on what they perceived as needing to be changed to improve student achievement. I also began delegating more responsibilities to increase the foundation of leadership in our school.
>
> *Priscilla McKnight*, Midland City Elementary School

Each of the principals engaged in a running dialogue with their staffs in an effort to determine the best solutions for the most meaningful problems. The dialogue took many forms, but all resulted in honest and open communication. Once again, shared leadership led to the identification of solutions that would have been unlikely without group input.

In some instances, the simple step of including the staff in framing the school improvement process energized the school. Clearly, those who contribute meaningfully have a greater stake in the outcome.

All initial phases of prioritizing for improvement—honest self- assessment, increased communication, solicitation of input—widen and deepen the foundation of leadership in the school. Simple physics tells us that a strong foundation lends stability to any object. Once again, we find that school improvement starts with improving the adults, here specifically improving the shared leadership in the school.

Change occurs more readily when staff and faculty stand behind it, and even more readily when they share in leading it. However, that cannot occur in an environment filled with rancor or distrust. Several of the principals stated that their next priority, after determining the problems, was to build trusting relationships with the staff. Recognizing the need for collective effort by a leadership team, they nurtured the environment in which that effort would thrive.

Road Maps for Change

> It just seemed like common sense that to get people to want to work together for change they have to trust you and believe that you trust them. So I started by developing positive relationships and helping people believe in themselves as good teachers.
>
> *LaVeral Graf*, W. C. Griggs Elementary School

> I asked for input from everyone and made sure everyone knew what decisions were made. Once a decision was determined, it was made clear that everyone was expected to abide by it.
>
> *Betty J. Warren*, Huxford Elementary School

> Our first priority was the staff because I believe that they are the key to student learning.
>
> *Scott Glasrud*, Southwest Secondary Learning Center

> We really emphasized our school vision and encouraged individuals to share their visions for the school as well.
>
> *Rebecca Miller*, Highland Elementary School

> We simply looked at the new state standards and determined which changes would have the greatest positive impact on student achievement.
>
> *Charles Kyle*, Haines Middle School

The school leaders who contributed to this book shared the goal of meeting the needs of all students, but they faced a wide variety of challenges. As they decided what to do first, many chose to start where they knew they could make a difference right away.

Recognizing that some problems take longer than others to address, they resisted the temptation to tackle school improvement on too broad a front. Prioritized change in a clearly planned sequence brought better results than major upheavals without sufficient forethought.

Finally, they never gave up. Step by step, little by little, day by day, and year by year, they kept moving forward on their journey to school improvement.

Nothing in the world can take the place of persistence.

Talent will not; nothing is more common than the unsuccessful with great talent.

Genius will not; unrewarded genius is almost a proverb.

Education will not; the world is full of educated derelicts.

Persistence and determination alone are omnipotent.

Calvin Coolidge

To reach the needs of all students, a school must prioritize its efforts—and persist until it reaches its goals.

> When I was in the classrooms, I noticed that the lessons did not seem to have any sequence and were not related to the standards. I believe that lessons need to be driven by student needs and standards. My school leadership team and I met weekly to determine a way to improve the connectedness of the lessons. The assessment binders were a product of those early meetings.
>
> *Deborah Lazio*, Chester Dewey School #14

> I asked a lot of questions and really listened to the answers. I looked at the data. But first, I saw how depressing our dull gray walls were and decided we had to brighten the place up.
>
> *Dale Hancock*, Dutton School

> Each year I chipped away at things to improve. The key was to do a few things well and not attempt to do everything at once and end up doing them poorly.
>
> *Judy Knotts*, St. Gabriel's Catholic School

> I worked to ensure that students and faculty could recognize patterns. That could only come with the development of consistency in the daily processes. We eliminated confusion.
>
> *Lynn Ritvo*, Former School Principal
> Alabama State Department of Education

> We used a Pareto approach to determining the 20 percent high need/high leverage areas to improve.
>
> *Cliff Downey*, Mooroopna Park Primary School

Chapter Summary

We asked the leaders of effective schools how they managed the journey to school improvement. Most of them viewed honest self-assessment as the crucial starting point. They emphasized the need for shared leadership to move change forward. Resisting the temptation to take on too much at once, they started where they could make the most difference, proceeded with a series of carefully planned efforts, and kept on going until they reached their goal.

Part III

Conclusion:
If We Had Our Way

10

The Road Ahead[1]

A people who mean to be their own governors must arm themselves with all the power which knowledge gives.

Thomas Jefferson

---

1 The authors are indebted to the Southern Regional Education Board (SREB), whose work throughout the Southeast and indeed the nation has shown that a comprehensive approach to educational reform is the only way to create systemic school improvement. Many of the ideas in this concluding section are supported by their research.

If America is to flourish in the 21st century, we must do a better job of educating *all* our children. As a first step, we must reject the notions that some children can achieve and others cannot, that some students deserve to graduate and others do not. Dropping out is nondiscriminatory; its problems don't start or stop at the city line, the poverty line, or the color line. As long as we accept the myth that dropouts are inevitable, students will fall by the wayside. We must replace this long-ingrained myth with the new conviction that dropping out is unacceptable—an insidious disease that affects not only students but also parents, teachers, and communities—and we must act on that conviction.

Many believe that if we ignore the problem of at-risk students, it will go away. But American society keeps evolving, and its pressures and instabilities have only intensified the dilemma. The heated debates about illegal immigrants underscore just one aspect of its challenges.

And yet, some schools succeed where others fail. The truly effective schools, many of which we highlight in this book, have a single trait in common: They keep working to improve; they keep striving to meet the needs of all their students. Their efforts rest on honest self-assessment, critical research regarding new teaching theory, and dedication to doing what is best for children. That does not happen by accident. It requires sound leadership.

Great Expectations

Faster than a speeding bullet. More powerful than a locomotive. Able to leap tall buildings in a single bound.

We expect our educational leaders to possess superhuman qualities: unstinting devotion to instructional leadership; firm discipline in raising standards; sensitivity to culturally and ethnically diverse students; and the ability to focus on staff empowerment, family involvement, and community collaboration all at the same time. We imagine that they have unbounded energy, unlimited hours in the day. We want them to do it all. Well, principals and school superintendents can't do it all; but with effective training, solid support through mentoring, and greater resources, they can do a great deal.

Preparing Future School Leaders

The No Child Left Behind Act has made it necessary for leader preparation programs to work with the local education agencies that they serve. The partnership must go much deeper. The programs that prepare our leaders—and, for that matter, our teachers—must become clinical in nature. They must do their teaching in the environment of school.

Educational leaders today need to arm themselves with more than knowledge. To fully tap its power, they must learn how to apply that knowledge in a real-world setting. This requires the development of partnerships between colleges of education and local education agencies. It requires the identification of *training schools* for interns, analogous to the *training hospitals* where future physicians hone their skills. Although that may sound improbable, such programs already exist for teachers at Trinity University, the University of Southern Maine, the University of California at Berkeley, and the University of Virginia.

The release of Arthur Levine's *Educating School Leaders* (2005), a report on the quality of university preparation programs for school leaders, stands as a milestone in the campaign to better prepare instructional leaders. The report stated that the quality of university preparation programs ranges from "inadequate" to "appalling." Dr. Levine, president of Teacher's College at Columbia University at the time the report was published, provided this indictment of leadership programs in 2005. The report highlighted the problems of an irrelevant curriculum, low admission and graduation standards, weak faculty, inadequate clinical instruction, inappropriate degrees, and poor research. Unfortunately, although there is much talk about reform, few real changes appear to be in the offing.

A New Direction

Many leadership preparation programs today have very little connection with the reality of today's educational environment. In effect, they train people to lead schools that no longer exist. When their graduates walk through real doors into real schools, they find themselves woefully unprepared for the variety of problems they encounter.

If we had our way, university preparation programs would prepare instructional leaders very differently than they do now. The first significant new direction should be that kindergarten through grade 12 (K–12) and higher education collaborate at every juncture of the candidate's preparation. Schools and districts should have the ability to nominate potential leaders who they feel have the attributes to be successful in leadership positions. It makes no sense that higher education prepares leaders without those who will ultimately do the hiring. An advisory group consisting of the local education authority and the university must plan the preparation program together.

Universities point to their work with K–12 schools for intern placement as collaboration enough. We argue that collaboration between the university and K–12 should start with the selection of potential candidates and the admissions process, extend through course design and course evaluation, and culminate with the internship and evaluation of the program in general.

If we had our way, admission to university preparation programs would require an interview conducted by a committee that includes both K–12 instructional leaders and higher education faculty. The interviewers should ask specific questions about the applicant's past work, goals, and instructional experiences. Having people at the table who may be the candidate's future employer adds a *real-world* dimension to the admissions process. More importantly, a potential employer knows what the future employee must know and be able to do. Although we believe that self-selection should remain an option for candidates entering a preparation program, research shows that when the candidate is tapped by a school system and supported with the possibility of employment, preparation is more meaningful.

If we had our way, the college curriculum would be heavily weighted toward instructional leadership rather than administrative leadership. Although educators have been saying this for years, universities have been extremely slow to change. Dr. Levine describes the typical course of study as little more than a grab bag of survey classes—such as historical and philosophical foundations of education, educational psychology, and research methods—with little or no relevance to the job of leading instruction and improving student achievement (2005). Courses in how to plan for continuous improvement, recognize quality teaching and learning, and attract and maintain the finest teaching staff must replace the survey classes.

If we had our way, universities would employ both K–12 adjunct practitioners and university instructors to guide the preparation of future instructional leaders. Too many university instructors are too far removed from the day-to-day operations of a school. Candidates in instructional leadership preparation programs must benefit from purposeful *hands-on* experiences that prepare them to lead the essential work of school improvement. Instructional leadership is learned through studying the key concepts and skills used by effective leaders, observing good models, studying accepted best practices and benchmarks from other schools and districts (and from industry), and experiencing the reality of trial and error in the workplace.

Courses throughout the preparation program should have clinical parts that take candidates into schools to experience real day-to-day problems with students in the building and touching on every aspect of school leadership. Planning an internship experience must again involve the university and K–12. Careful consideration must be given to candidate placement with qualified mentors in the field. Standards and remuneration should be high for the professionals who take on interns.

If we had our way, internship programs would design an explicit set of school-based assignments that provide opportunities to apply the knowledge, skills, attitudes, and practices of school leadership. These assignments should address the core responsibilities of a school leader, as identified in state standards and research, and be incorporated in the university preparation programs' design. A developmental continuum of practice would start with observing critical school-based activities, then participating in and leading them, with analysis, synthesis, and evaluation of real-life problems at each level.

Field placements provide opportunities to work with diverse students, teachers, parents, and communities. Program faculty with the expertise and time to give frequent formative feedback on interns' performance provide ongoing supervision. Rigorous evaluations of interns' performance of core school leader responsibilities are based on consistent procedures and clearly defined performance standards and exit criteria.

Only when universities and K–12 work collaboratively to train future instructional leaders can we hope to meet the needs of tomorrow's students. Arthur Levine's report is catalyst enough for all parties to take this challenge seriously.

11

The Road Map to Improvement

Everything that is really great and inspiring is created by the individual who is allowed to labor in freedom.

Albert Einstein

Although we consider improving the training of prospective school leaders vital, we have focused throughout this book on what leaders already on the job can do. In this chapter, we offer suggestions, some more concrete and others more ambitious, for ways to keep America's schools moving forward.

Building Improvement into the School

We cannot overemphasize the goal of improving student achievement in every classroom, in every school. To work toward that goal, we must build improvement into the very structure of school.

Highlight the Supportive Role of Leadership

Principals, grade leaders, and (in middle and high schools) department chairs must help new teachers—both those new to the system and those new to the school. There are several ways to do this. In one school we know, the principal scheduled all new teachers with a common lunch period. This provided an opportunity for them to sit around the lunch table and share common concerns dealing with classroom management, assessments, standards, student achievement, and curriculum. This process worked better when master teachers were able to sit in on these lunchroom meetings.

Every Friday, the principal scheduled a lunch meeting with these new people and provided them with condensed versions of professional journals and books and then discussed them. The entire process was meant to engender an environment where learning was expected and the tools necessary for that to occur were welcomed. Not only must schools provide the tools necessary to succeed, they must provide the environment in which their use is appropriate. Even the best tools are of little use in the hands of the unwilling.

Practice Classroom Intervisitation

Groups of master teachers selected by department or grade could make classroom visits to nontenured colleagues and offer suggestions or assistance. These visits are less daunting than a visit from a supervisor or other rating officer. Likewise, master teachers could invite novices to observe their teaching techniques. Principals could offer to teach classes and have them videotaped for discussion at faculty or department meetings.

Maximize Faculty Meetings

Principals can identify master teachers, counselors, and other support personnel to share success stories detailing adaptable practices involving student attendance, behavioral procedures, curriculum overlap, and state accountability measures. However, the ultimate goal of every faculty meeting must be improvement of student learning. To that end, faculty meeting should always include a discussion of student data and the practices necessary to improve that data.

Boost Grade-Level and Department Meetings

Where possible, new individuals teaching at the same grade level or in the same department should have common planning periods to discuss common experiences, concerns, successes, and challenges. The end product of those discussions should be the identification of practices and strategies that have been proven to increase student achievement.

Focus on Internal Staff Development

Each school should build a cadre of concerned, influential, and involved individuals who come together to generate improvement ideas, identify internal resources for professional development, or tap outside experts to help with improving assessment scores, attendance, parent or community involvement, or other areas. This working improvement group should represent all stakeholders: parents, the outside community, and the internal stakeholders. Principals must provide the time, space, and other resources to support this group.

Value Highly Qualified and Highly Effective Teachers

We have all had teachers who knew their material (highly qualified) but couldn't convey it to students (not highly effective). No Child Left Behind provisions and increased state standards require both highly qualified *and* highly effective teachers. This mandate poses a greater challenge in a classroom of students with wide-ranging backgrounds and abilities.

Guarantee Sufficient Time for Training

Most educators agree that their most precious commodity is time. Teachers never have enough time to think, reflect, plan, discuss student needs with their colleagues, and talk about what works and what doesn't. To keep effective teachers in the profession, and to keep teachers in the profession effective, we must integrate that time into the school calendar.

Make Schools Student Friendly

We need schools that welcome students, value them as individuals, and convince them that they can reach their full potential through education. We need schools committed to the belief that no child should be allowed to fail, regardless of cultural, economic, social, or other obstacles. And we need schools that let go of rigid time constraints for student learning. Why should algebra class stop after 48 minutes? Why must earning a high school diploma take 4 years, not 2 or 8? What is so sacrosanct about summer vacation? We need schools that teach *all* students for as long as it takes for them to succeed, and do it well.

Building Improvement Into the System

Many school leaders have the autonomy to implement the steps outlined above in their own schools. But policymakers at the district, state, and national level must do their part to build the goal of improving student achievement into our educational system as a whole.

Align Our System

The K–16 school system does not operate as a system but rather as isolated, independent units that frequently do not talk or relate to one another. This limits the ability to maximize performance at every level. This disconnect shows up, for example, in criticism at the postsecondary level of graduates from the kindergarten through grade 12 (K–12) system. Colleges and universities complain that students entering their doors aren't prepared to deal with college-level work. They say that they have to provide remediation for large numbers of students.

By aligning the K–12 system with the college and university system, we could increase the effectiveness and the potential of all. Colleges and universities could validate the importance of high school diplomas by refusing to admit students who do not perform at the level they expect. They could maintain contact with K–12 administrators and students to keep their expectations front and center.

Share the Responsibility

Schools cannot and should not bear all of the responsibility for the failure of students to achieve. Some students enter school years behind in reading, writing, and other skills. Although school programs can overcome family influences to close achievement gaps where they exist, it would greatly speed up the process if families assumed some of the burden. We need families involved in the learning process from kindergarten through high school.

Eliminate the At-Risk Curriculum

Traditionally, schools have tracked students into college preparation, vocational-technical training, and *other*. In the low-level *other* curriculum, we find general math, general science, communications, and other courses without much content; and there we also find the at-risk students. This curriculum gives credit for seat time not for authentic learning. It prepares students neither for college nor for the world of work but for a world that no longer exists. Such programs do students a disservice, demean the profession of teaching, and have no place in public schools.

Enhance Accountability and Assessment

Tests today are used to place blame and expose weaknesses in curriculum, textbooks, and teaching practices. A systemic approach toward reform is more effective than piecemeal stopgap solutions. Systemic reform efforts must show clear direction in meeting the demands of the state, local community, and the federal government. But these efforts rely on local initiative. School systems must coordinate across elementary, middle, and high school levels to ensure compatibility and avoid teaching the same thing over and over.

Most current reforms consist of standards and assessments. They are punitive in nature, targeting those who fail to achieve. They offer little in the way of strategies for achieving success and changing school culture. They provide no additional resources or assistance to low-performing schools. Policymakers demand quick results, but school improvement cannot be achieved overnight and frequently takes longer to have an impact than originally planned.

Put Standardized Tests in Perspective

Currently, high-stakes testing is the measure most used to evaluate the success of schools, teachers, and students. But standardized tests are imperfect measures of the situation at a particular time. Jim Honan, Harvard

University's educational cochair of the Institute for Educational Management and faculty member at the Harvard Graduate School of Education, makes the point that "schools are movies, not snapshots." Dr. Honan urges care in making swift evaluative decisions based on only part of the picture.

Used properly, standardized tests can be one useful, albeit imperfect, tool among many to assist teachers and schools in meeting student needs. But we do not always use them properly, and that can have serious consequences. Standardized tests measure only a tiny fraction of the many gifts, talents, and *ways to be smart* our children present to the world; and even that fraction they measure very imperfectly. A single test cannot sum up a child or a school. Using test scores to arrive at judgments about students, teachers, and schools is a very tricky business. Many social, cultural, and economic factors far beyond the teachers' control have an enormous impact on those scores.

And yet, as long as high-stakes standardized testing receives such heavy emphasis across the nation, school leaders must take steps to align what is taught with what will be tested. Otherwise, they allow their schools to put their students at risk of failure.

Choose Leaders From Within the Field

Faced with a shortage of up-and-coming leaders in education, some have suggested looking outside the field, possibly to industry or the military, for candidates. Granted, talented individuals in either field could make the leap into education. But we oppose this approach as a general recruitment tool, and the data bear us out. Would a hospital hire an administrator who lacked knowledge in the field? Would a business seeking to improve its bottom line recruit an outsider with no business experience? Why do we sell short the difficult job of running educational institutions?

If we want to boost recruitment, we should pay current and future school leaders more. The U.S. Air Force knows that it spends $1,000,000 to train a pilot, and it pays its pilots well because retention is more cost-effective than replacement. Why not apply the same principle to school leaders?

Consider Spending More Money

Although money cannot relieve all our educational system's woes, the United States cannot afford to spend more money (per individual) on incarceration than on education—especially when the U.S. Department of Justice tells us that 72% of all prisoners failed to graduate high school. We must pay teachers, principals, and superintendents a salary commensurate with their responsibilities. Those who compare America's schools with those of foreign countries should also compare statistics on the salaries paid to educators (as a percentage of the nation's gross domestic product). Value in America is frequently measured by income. It is shameful that people with less education, working in occupations with less responsibility, earn more than the people who educated them. It is time for our *education* presidents, senators, governors, and representatives to put their money where their mouths are.

Build the nation's stock of educational leaders. At the end of World War II, Congress created the GI Bill of Rights. Within 7 years, approximately 8 million returning veterans seized the opportunity to enroll in colleges and universities. This yielded a cohort of higher-income, greater-educated, better-trained individuals. Perhaps our nation should launch a similar initiative to build our stock of future school leaders.

12

A Dream, a Plan

The principals of tomorrow's schools must be instructional leaders who possess the requisite skills, capacities, and commitment to lead the accountability parade, not follow it. Excellence in school leadership should be recognized as the most important component of school reform. Without leadership, the chances for systemic improvement in teaching and learning are nil.

Gerald N. Tirozzi
Executive Director, NASSP

Every educator dreams of one day being able to fix all that is wrong with our schools by building on all that is right. In this chapter, we present our dream—a comprehensive plan for coherent professional development for instructional leaders in our nation's public schools.

Countless studies indicate that high-quality, research-based professional development must be available to support school leaders if they are to lead improved student achievement. States invest millions of dollars in professional development each year. But the following concerns exist in most states:

- The content of a *continuum of professional development* driven by standards for instructional leaders does not exist in many states or should be updated.

- Very few states have unified structures with the capacity to develop, or ensure delivery of, learning experiences that support and sustain the attainment of leadership standards.

- Tools and processes that enable leaders to assess their needs in light of the standards for instructional leaders are rarely in place. Few if any tools and processes are in place to address both individual goals and the context in which the leader is working to increase academic achievement for all students.

- No structure exists to ensure that instructional leaders can engage in a seamless system that eliminates duplication and gaps. Furthermore, no structure exists to ensure that professional development of leaders meets high standards of quality in content, delivery, and results.

- Funding and time to develop and support the ongoing professional development of instructional leaders are usually grossly inadequate. This lack of resources for leadership development is exacerbated by insufficient collaboration among private, public, and educational entities.

The idea that school is the center of teacher education is built on the realization that whatever teachers become professionally, the process is not finished when they complete their teacher education program at 21. Learning to teach well is a lifetime endeavor.

Elliot W. Eisner,
Stanford University

Our Plan for Leadership Development

We offer here a concrete proposal for a state-level system of professional development for instructional leaders. The plan embraces 12 essential elements:

1. Every state would develop a council for leadership development to work with entities both inside and outside state departments of education to provide advisement for a seamless system of professional development for instructional leaders. The professional development sanctioned by this council would constitute the Professional Learning Units (PLUs) required for continued leadership certification.

2. Members of this council would be active practitioners who have distinguished themselves by leading sustained student achievement in their schools or systems and who meet the following criteria:

   - Five years of experience in the position represented on the council (superintendent, principal, assistant principal, teacher leader, system-level instructional staff, university school of education staff)
   - Documented success in the position represented, especially as it relates to improving student achievement or assisting others in improving student achievement
   - Willingness and capability to attend quarterly and/or called meetings of the council
   - Documented leadership in professional development design, delivery, and/or evaluation.

3. The mission of the Council for Leadership Development would be to design a continuum of leadership development in support of the state standards for instructional leaders based on the needs of instructional leaders.

4. The council would also sanction professional development to support this continuum and to be used for certification renewal. This professional development would be based on current research and best practices, would not be episodic, and would be free of gaps and redundancy. The council would seek to minimize the time school leaders are away from their schools or offices, while maximizing the effect of research-based quality professional development to ensure improved student achievement. The council would place emphasis on professional development that places school leaders into effective teams, collaboratively seeking to improve student achievement.

5. The council would focus on the annual professional development for the following groups of instructional leaders:
   - Superintendents
   - System instructional staff
   - Veteran principals
   - New principals
   - Assistant principals
   - Aspiring principals
   - Teacher leaders

6. Approval of the continuum of leadership development would ensure that the professional development focuses primarily on improved student achievement through improved leadership.

7. The council would annually review the continuum using the most current research on professional development to ensure the appropriateness of professional development for the target audiences.

8. The council would ensure that the professional development offered addresses needs garnered from an annual needs assessment, student achievement data, and state, regional, and national research on best practices.

9. The council would establish criteria that professional development activities must meet in order to be granted PLU status.

10. The council would develop, issue, and review requests for professional development proposals (RFPs) from the State Department of Education, local education agencies, regional in-service centers, universities, regional education laboratories, state professional associations, and others to meet the needs of instructional leaders as determined by the annual needs assessment and the continuum. It would sanction a calendar for leadership professional development that indicates windows of opportunity for professional development to be offered, but which also indicates *blackout* times when certain audiences are unavailable (e.g., during state testing or on traditional dates for state meetings).

11. The council would meet quarterly to review professional development proposals and to sanction professional development activities that meet the criteria for PLU status and that may be used for certification renewal.

12. The council would oversee the approval of professional development and determination of the appropriate target audience.

A process like the one described previously would exist in every state, ensuring once and for all that professional development for instructional leaders is coherent, comprehensive and meaningful.

Improving the preparation of leaders and building improvement into the system are vital to improving our schools so that they better meet the needs of at-risk students. The contents of this book do provide a theoretical framework for addressing those needs. There is one overriding question that ultimately must be answered if theory is to become practice. That question emanates from the following poem:

> *All men dream; but not equally.*
> *Those who dream by the night in the dusty*
> *Recesses of their minds*
> *Awake to find that it was vanity;*
> *But the dreamers of day are dangerous men,*
> *That they may act their dreams with open*
> *Eyes to make it possible.*
>
> T.E. Lawrence

What is your dream for your at-risk students? What do you see for your school when you become one of the *dreamers of day*? It is vital to make those dreams public and to enlist the help of the faculty, the staff, families, and the surrounding community to build them into your school. We must move our dreams from the ephemeral realm of wishful thinking into the concrete world of a legitimate plan. A manager can keep a school running smoothly, but it takes a leader to convey a vision and to energize a staff. It takes a leader to guide a school to victory over ignorance and stupidity. For the sake of students everywhere, we wish you much success on that journey from at risk to excellence.

Appendix I

Nationwide Survey Questions

Please answer the following questions as completely as possible. Add additional sheets if necessary. Thank you for your input and for your efforts on behalf of your students.

1. To what instructional and/or organizational strategies do you attribute the high achievement of your students?

2. Research has shown that leadership's effect on student achievement is second only to classroom instruction. What *specific* practices or actions have *you* taken to boost student achievement?

3. When you began your tenure as the school leader at your school, what were the first things you changed or upgraded?

4. Describe the process you used to determine how to prioritize the changes outlined in question 3.

5. In your role as school leader, what aspect of your job do you see as having the greatest effect on student achievement?

6. In your role as school leader, what do you see as critical to increasing the achievement level of your at-risk students?

7. How have you been able to promote stronger ties among your school staff?

8. How have you been able to promote stronger ties between the school and your students?

9. How have you been able to promote stronger ties between the school and the community?

I would like my school to be acknowledged in your book (*please check one*).

☐ Yes
☐ No

If yes is checked, please complete the following demographics section.

School Name: _____

School Address: _____

School Contact E-mail: _____

School Phone #: _____

School Website (if any): _____

School Leader(s): _____

_____

_____

Appendix II
Survey Participants

Bill Aaron
Asbury High School
1990 Asbury Road
Albertville, AL 35951
256-878-4068

Vonda Beaty
Townley Junior High School
62 Townley School Road
Townley, AL 35587

David Besile
R.B. Stall High School
7749 Pinehurst Street
Charleston, SC 29420
843-764-2200

Cyndi Brooks
Childersburg Elementary
235 Pinecrest Drive
Childersburg, AL 35044

Steve Brown
Council Elementary
1400 Avenue M Ensley
Birmingham, AL 35218

Sandra Byrd
McDavid-Jones Elementary
16250 Highway 45 South
Citronelle, AL   36522

Linda Cheryl Chapman
Saint Elmo Elementary
P.O. Box 250
St. Elmo, AL 36568
251-957-6314

Tammy Coefield
Fruithurst Elementary
222 School Street
Fruithurst, AL 36262

Nancy Croley
Walnut Park Elementary
3200 Walnut Street
Gadsden, AL 35901

W. Garry Derossett
Boone Grove High School
260 South 500 West
Valparaiso, IN 46385
219-988-4481

Cliff Downey
Mooroopna Park Primary School
P.O. Box 609, Mooroopna Victoria
Australia 3629
613-582-53856

Scott Glasrud
Southwest Secondary Learning
Center
10301 Candelaria Road NE
Albuquerque, NM 87112
505-296-7677

LeVeral Graf
Griggs Elementary School
6001 Three Notch Road
Mobile, AL 36619
251-221-1330

Susan Hair
Big Brothers/Big Sisters
1500 N. Second Street, Suite H
Harrisburg, PA 17102
717-236-0199

Dale Hancock
Dutton School
180 Main Street
Dutton, AL 35744
256-228-4265

Lagaylis Harbuck
Calcedeaver Elementary School
20185 Richard Weaver Road
Mount Vernon, AL 36560
251-221-1092

Steven Havens
Saltillo Elementary
424 South 3rd Street
Saltillo, MS 38866
662-869-3195

Gary Hughes
Cloverdale Elementary
303 Rollins Avenue
Dothan, AL 36301

Judy Knotts
St. Gabriel's Catholic School
2500 Wimberly Lane
Austin, TX 78735
512-327-7755

Patricia Kornegay
Highland Avenue Elementary
2024 Highland Avenue
Montgomery, AL 36107
334-269-3690

Charles Kyle
Haines Middle School
305 South 9th Street
St. Charles, IL 60174
630-377-4825

Deborah Lazio
Chester Dewey School #14
200 University Avenue
Rochester, NY 14605
585-325-6738

Mark Linton
Geneseo Elementary School
4050 Avon Road
Geneseo, NY 14454
585-243-3450

Susan Loftin
Heard Elementary
201 Daniel Circle
Dothan, AL 36301

Clairessa Love
Westview Elementary
1012 Ingersoll Drive
Phenix City, AL 36867

Priscilla McKnight
Midland City Elementary School
P.O. Box 1110
Midland City, AL 36350
334-983-4591

Mary Jo McLaughlin
The Academy of Creative Education
10333 Broadway
San Antonio, TX 78217
210-657-8970

Elmer Magyar
New Directions Alternative School
Manassas, VA

Lee Mansell
Foley Intermediate School
2000 South Cedar Street
Foley, AL 36535
251-943-1244

Linda Maxwell
Oak Mountain Intermediate
5486 Caldwell Mill Road
Birmingham, AL 35242

Rebecca Miller
Highland Elementary
3156 Tabor Road
Gadsden, AL 35904
256-546-7409

Sheila Newkirk-Squire
Buehrle Alternative School
426 E. Clay Street
Lancaster, PA 17602
717-291-6232

Karen Petersen
Northside Alternative Middle
School
5223 Blessing Street
San Antonio, TX 78228

Ronnie Poole
Athens Elementary School
515 N. Madison Street
Athens, AL 35611

Luann Rice
J.E. Turner Elementary
8361 Lott Road
Wilmer, AL 36587

Mike Rodgers
Jones Chapel Elementary
192 County Road 940
Cullman, AL 36262

Larry Sholes
Attucks Alternative Academy
346 S. 4th
Vinita, OK 74301
918-256-6470

Pat Sievers
    Ankeny Community Schools
    306 SW School Street
    Ankeny, IA 50021
    515-965-9600

Bruce Smith
    Albuquerque Charter Vocational
    High School
    1011 Lamberton N.E.
    Albuquerque, NM 87107
    505-341-0888

Eric Smith
    West Jasper Elementary
    1400 West 19th Street
    Jasper, AL 35501
    205-384-4311

Julie Stoneburner
    Ankeny Community Schools
    306 SW School Street
    Ankeny, IA 50021
    515-965-9600

Richard Storm
    Union Alternative School
    5656 S. 129th E. Avenue
    Tulsa, OK   74134
    918-459-6555

Suzann Tibbs
    Bluff City Elementary
    333 State Docks Road
    Eufaula, AL 36027

Agnes (Terri) Tomlinson
    George Hall Elementary
    1108 Antwerp Street
    Mobile, AL 36605-4856
    251-221-1345

Richard Varrati
    New Philadephia City Schools
    248 Front Avenue, SW
    New Philadelphia, OH 44663
    330-364-0600

Betty J. Warren
    Huxford Elementary School
    P.O. Box 10
    Huxford, AL 36543
    251-294-5475

Jessie Warren
    Western Heights Elementary
    520 Pump Station Road
    Eufaula, AL 36027
    334-687-1140

Linda Welch
    Whittier School
    536 Hill
    Downers Grove, IL 60515
    630-719-5865

Lisa Williams
    Peter Alba Elementary
    14180 Wintzell Avenue
    Bayou La Batre, AL 36509

Appendix III

Alabama's Torchbearer Schools: A Beacon of Hope

Read 10 good articles describing 10 "effective" schools and you will have read little about effective programs and a great deal about effective people. These schools "work" because the people driving them are able. Nothing else, ultimately, is very important.

Theodore R. Sizer, Founder,
Coalition of Essential Schools

Starting with the 2004–2005 school year, the Alabama Leadership Academy in the Alabama State Department of Education launched the Torchbearers program as a way to recognize high-poverty public schools in Alabama that have overcome odds and stand out as high-achievement schools. Schools considered for recognition have met the following criteria:

- At least 70% of the student population receives free/reduced price meals.

- At least 70% of the students score at level II or Level IV (proficient) on all sections of the Alabama Reading and Mathematics Test.

- Average percentile stands above 50 in reading and in mathematics on Stanford 10.

- At least 98% of grade 12 students pass all required subjects of the Alabama High School Graduation Examination.

- Average dropout rate is below the state average.

- School receives an ACT grade of C or above on state report card.

In the first year, 13 elementary schools earned recognition as Torchbearers. In the 2005–2006 school year, the program expanded to include high schools, and 22 schools made the list. Five schools from the previous year did not maintain their Torchbearer status; three of the schools changed leaders.

The principals of the first 13 Torchbearer schools were asked to complete a survey about their school (see box). The survey presented positive statements about autonomy, goals, faculty, assessment/achievement, and culture/climate. Principals indicated their degree of agreement with each statement. Those who gave strong positive responses in a category were invited to elaborate, and all were asked to specify qualities and practices that made their school effective.

Torchbearer Schools Principal Survey

Scale

1	=	strongly disagree	3	=	agree
2	=	disagree	4	=	strongly agree

Autonomy

1. I am allowed to make most important decisions on my own. 1 2 3 4

2. I have complete control over hiring of teachers and staff. 1 2 3 4

3. I am allowed to make instructional improvement decisions. 1 2 3 4

4. I am allowed to make all school-level budget decisions. 1 2 3 4

5. Central office staff members support my decisions. 1 2 3 4

If your total score on questions 1–5 is 15 or greater, please explain how your autonomy impacts student achievement in your school. If not, please proceed to question 6.

Goals

6. Goals and expectations are very clearly explained to parents. 1 2 3 4

7. Goals and expectations are very clearly explained to students. 1 2 3 4

8. My goals and expectations are shared by the staff and faculty. 1 2 3 4

9. All my students are capable of learning at a high level. 1 2 3 4

10. The goals of this school are tangible and measurable. 1 2 3 4

If your total score on questions 6–10 is 15 or greater, please explain how your (school's) goals and expectations impact student achievement in your school. If not, please proceed to question 11.

Faculty

11.	The teachers on my faculty are highly qualified.	1	2	3	4
12.	The teachers on my faculty are teaching within their field.	1	2	3	4
13.	I usually experience very little turnover on my faculty.	1	2	3	4
14.	My faculty has uniformly high expectations of their students.	1	2	3	4
15.	My faculty communicates effectively with one another.	1	2	3	4
16.	My faculty is constantly looking for better methods of teaching.	1	2	3	4
17.	My faculty meets regularly to discuss student achievement issues.	1	2	3	4
18.	My faculty is enthusiastic about teaching children.	1	2	3	4

If your total score on questions 11–18 is 24 or greater, please explain how your faculty impacts student achievement at your school. If not, please proceed to question 19.

Assessment and Achievement

19.	Our students' academic progress is assessed on a regular basis.	1	2	3	4
20.	Parents are regularly updated concerning student achievement.	1	2	3	4
21.	Testing is used as a diagnostic tool for improvement in my school.	1	2	3	4
22.	Student testing reveals teaching proficiency as well as student knowledge.	1	2	3	4
23.	As instructional leader, I personally insure that students are regularly tested.	1	2	3	4
24.	Standardized tests accurately gauge our school's success.	1	2	3	4
25.	My school actively practices for standardized tests.	1	2	3	4

If your total score on questions 19–25 is 21 or greater, please explain what impact that student assessment has had on student achievement in your school. If not, please proceed to question 26.

Culture and Climate

26.	Parents are actively involved in our school activities.	1	2	3	4
27.	There are very few discipline problems in my school.	1	2	3	4
28.	Effective teachers minimize discipline problems.	1	2	3	4
29.	My faculty addresses and values the cultural differences in their classroom.	1	2	3	4
30.	Character education is an important part of the curriculum at my school.	1	2	3	4
31.	Cleanliness is expected and valued in my school.	1	2	3	4
32.	Teachers respect students in my school.	1	2	3	4
33.	My school is a safe place for students.	1	2	3	4

If your total score on questions 26–33 is 24 or greater, please explain what impact the climate and culture of your school has had on student achievement. If not, please proceed to question 34.

34. What qualities or practices do you think make your school effective where other schools with similar demographics are not? Please be explicit.

———————————————————

Researchers analyzed their responses to determine means, standard errors, and variances. They also made site visits to corroborate the survey results and discern why Torchbearers outperformed other schools with similar demographics. Their objective was to identify the characteristics Torchbearer schools had in common, reasoning that the practices and skills contributing to their success could benefit other schools.

The site visits were invaluable. The 13 schools exhibited several traits in common. The most striking commonality was children who were excited about learning. However, each school also had distinctive characteristics. Each excelled in its own way; taken together, they exemplify what people can achieve when they truly believe that they can make a difference.

Torchbearer Schools: Shared Core Values

The following sections highlight the similarities in approach and attitude that the survey and site visits revealed, along with many of the specific comments voiced by school leaders, teachers, staff, and students. The Torchbearers manifested a remarkable commitment to the educational process and to the wellbeing of their children. Two details exemplify that commitment.

One is the very simple motto of the Dutton School, "Where Learning Matters." The second is the observation that at Huxford Elementary School, the principal told every class and every teacher how deeply she cared for them.

Autonomy

One of the key strengths of Torchbearer schools is that their leaders have autonomy, in particular the freedom to make instructional decisions in their schools. The mean score for statement 3, "I am allowed to make instructional improvement decisions," was 3.92 (on a scale of 1 to 4). The responses to statement 5, "Central office staff members support my decisions," yielded a similar statistic. These scores indicate that principals of Torchbearer schools can address student achievement issues specific to their school. Couple that autonomy with shared leadership, a practice widely used in Torchbearer schools, and the result is decision making by the adults who know most about the road to student achievement: the teachers. This autonomy makes it easier for schools to address existing problems, but it also enables them to anticipate and manage future challenges.

The autonomy enjoyed by the Torchbearer schools was most often earned, rather than freely given. However, it was also persistently solicited. Nine of the thirteen Torchbearer principals clearly believed that the progress in their schools often required them to take strong stances with both faculty and immediate supervisors. A group of teachers from Asbury High School went so far as to state, "We are a strong faculty who can do what we do because we know our principal will fight for this school and will fight for us if he knows we are right. That obligates us to do what is right because then we know he has our back."

Goals

The 13 Torchbearer schools hold high expectations for all their students. But what sets them apart from less effective schools is not that their goals are lofty but that they are also stubbornly down to earth. Every single principal responding to the survey strongly agreed with the statement, "The goals of this school are tangible and measurable."

Faculty

Every Torchbearer principal praised the school's faculty and staff:

- Dutton: "a dedicated group of professionals who love what they do and are willing to go above and beyond the norm to ensure that every child is successful"
- Highland Avenue Elementary School: "spectacular" and "inspirational"
- Midland City Elementary School: "dedicated and caring"

The principals uniformly described their faculty as enthusiastic about teaching children and constantly looking for better teaching methods. Such statements attest to the importance of an exemplary faculty. However, they also reflect the importance of a leader who recognizes and celebrates excellence.

Each Torchbearer school reported very little staff turnover. However, both the principals and the staff members interviewed described what turnover there had been as mostly positive:

- Calcedeaver Elementary School: "People leave if they don't fit in, and people don't fit in if they are not completely devoted to the students."
- Foley Intermediate School: "They work very hard together, and they make teachers who are unwilling to work uncomfortable to the point that they leave on their own."
- W. C. Griggs Elementary School: Two staff members said, "Teachers who are uncomfortable with data leave and find employment elsewhere."
- Highland Avenue: The faculty is a devoted group of professionals who "do not accept anything less than excellence from each other. People leave who cannot live up to that standard."

These are true professionals, holding self and others to a shared standard of excellence.

Leadership

Not surprisingly, the Torchbearer principals differed in their approaches to the job. Teachers say that Terri Tomlinson, the former principal of Maryvale, appears the happiest when she is teaching students or faculty something new that she has learned. She called herself the Chief Learning Officer. At Midland City Elementary, the principal visits every classroom every day; teachers stated that she often participates in teaching lessons.

Highland Avenue staff described their principal as a "dynamo" and lauded her for always trying to find new ways to get better. Huxford's principal runs the school as an extended family; its staff and students are extremely close and extremely loyal to one another. Teachers at Highland Elementary School described the principal as the "stern grandmotherly type who loves everyone implicitly but does not put up with anything that might hurt her kids." Dutton's principal, recalling that you lead, follow, or get out of the way, said he had "done all three because my faculty is much smarter than me." However, his faculty unanimously praised him. At W. C. Griggs Elementary, the principal is the ultimate technician who is supremely proficient and knowledgeable about assessments and the achievement level of her students. West Jasper Elementary School's principal very accurately described himself as the school's "#1 Cheerleader."

Assessment and Achievement

Student achievement takes center stage at Torchbearer schools. They rely heavily on assessment to determine how effectively they are addressing student needs. Every principal surveyed strongly agreed with statement 19, "Our students' academic progress is assessed on a regular basis"; statement 21, "Testing is used as a diagnostic tool for improvement in my school"; statement 22, "Student testing reveals teaching proficiency as well as student knowledge"; and statement 23, "As instructional leader, I personally ensure that students are regularly tested."

Student assessment drives student instruction. At Western Heights Elementary School, the principal stated, "Because of the amount of analysis of student data that we do, our teachers can allow their students to guide the instruction because it is based on student needs." At Saint Elmo Elementary School, "systematic, job-imbedded training…includes regularly scheduled data meetings," and "teachers are required to keep progress monitoring booklets on each student." The principals at West Jasper, Calcedeaver, Highland Avenue, Western Heights, W. C. Griggs, St. Elmo, Maryvale, Dutton, and Foley Intermediate all explicitly praised the work their teachers do in meetings to discuss student data and emphasized the value of the information garnered.

Site visitors found the importance of student achievement manifested in several interesting ways. For one thing, most bulletin boards feature student achievement and assessment data; and at six of the schools, *every* bulletin board highlights student achievement. At W. C. Griggs, every grade book has a copy of semester objectives laminated to the bottom of each page; each assignment and test must specify the objective it addresses. At Calcedeaver

Elementary, when a class goes to the library or the computer lab, that teacher pulls in students from another class for remediation, effectively doubling the amount of remediation that some students receive. At Huxford Elementary School, whenever students are standing in line—in the cafeteria, in the hallway waiting to use the restroom—they have a library book in hand and spend that time reading. At every school, the library was a hub of activity.

Culture and Climate

The Alabama schools recognized as Torchbearers have made a commitment to overcoming the odds stacked against the children they serve. Their culture revolves around children. Visitors see teachers busy with students, students engaged and on task—and smiling. Several principals indicated that their culture was productive and positive because their faculties were just as interested in learning better ways to teach as the students were in finding better ways to learn.

Nine of the Torchbearer schools offer both after- and before-school remediation. Children *and* parents are welcome to attend, and they show up in large numbers because the schools are safe and inviting. Every principal surveyed mentioned *safety* or *safe school* as a linchpin of their culture and their success. All agreed strongly with statement 33, "My school is a safe place for students." Calcedeaver's principal explained her insistence on a safe school: "We are a small school and everyone has a sense of family. You make sure that your family is safe." Many other schools echoed that sentiment and put it into practice. When the State Department of Education representative walked in for the site visit at Highland Avenue, he was met in the hallway and escorted to the Parents Resource Room, where two parent volunteers questioned him to determine if he belonged on campus. (One politely stated, "You look nice in your suit, but that doesn't mean you're supposed to be here.")

As safe and inviting places where students are continually engaged, the Torchbearer schools experience very few disciplinary problems. Furthermore, each principal strongly agreed with statement 28, "Effective teachers minimize discipline problems." West Jasper's principal underscored this: "I can only afford to be the #1 Cheerleader in this school because I have great teachers who are constantly teaching, and that keeps me from having to stay in the office dealing with discipline." That focus on strong teaching in the classroom underpins a positive school culture.

The Torchbearers excel because they have administrators and teachers who not only understand the science, but also embrace the art of teaching. In every case, the principals cited the faculty and staff as the mainstay of the school's success. Each faculty insisted that success would have been impossible without their principal's support and guidance. Furthermore, no one at the schools sees what they are doing as particularly out of the ordinary. In their minds, they are simply doing their jobs; but the way they do it somehow inspires and empowers their students.

Conclusion

Although school cultures notoriously resist change, they cannot hold it at bay. The 13 schools identified as Torchbearers work hard to keep change positive and purposeful. Foley Intermediate piloted a single-sex-classroom program as a way to increase student achievement. W. C. Griggs Elementary makes math classroom assignments fluid, moving students from class to class based on achievement levels and needs. When second graders at Western Heights struggled with reading, two fourth-grade teachers known as exceptional reading teachers agreed to move to the second grade. At West Jasper Elementary, five children from each class are identified for remediation at the start of each year. If one student tests out of the program, another takes the slot. Each of these examples underscores a simple truth: these schools are learning sites for students, faculty, and staff.

The Torchbearer schools differ in their programs, but they share two important traits: consistency of effort and purity of purpose. St. Elmo Elementary has an "Every Day Counts" calendar that ensures a steady, schoolwide focus on achievement. At Huxford Elementary, aides work every afternoon with students identified as strugglers. At W. C. Griggs, interventions take place from 8:00 to 8:30 every morning and small-group interventions from 2:30 to 3:00 every afternoon. Whatever they deem necessary for success, the Torchbearer schools practice it every day.

These schools and their leaders do everything with their students in mind. Several students at Asbury High School commented that this made them feel appreciated. Teachers at Calcedeaver Elementary School know that the principal bases each decision on what students need; she herself stated that although she truly values her staff, she was put there for the children's benefit. Highland Avenue's principal invites one student a day to read to her in her office—the "most precious time" of her day. She also insists on a spotless school; according to the custodian, she makes it clear that the children deserve it. The principal at Western Heights stated that the faculty knows he cares for them deeply, but they also know he *loves* the kids. West Jasper's principal calls himself the "#1 Cheerleader," and the teachers have *no* doubt that he is there for the kids. The omnipresent smiles and consistently caring attitudes observed at these schools substantiate that they are in the business of helping children learn.

The final question on the Torchbearers survey instrument asked, "What qualities or practices do you think make your school effective where other schools with similar demographics are not?" It is appropriate to end this section by presenting the principals' responses"

- Students and student needs drive our instruction. Everyone—teachers, students, custodians and support personnel—knows they are a part of our success.

- Some children receive intervention four or five times a day until they are able to improve.

- Our staff works very hard on special projects and special events. We want our students to know that we are special and they are important.

- We work to help each other across the curriculum. Our staff really works together, and our students see that.

- The dedication of the faculty and staff is *the* key. They have internalized our mission statement and challenge students to be their best.

- We have very caring and intelligent teachers and staff. We are determined to reach our shared, common goals.

- High-level, ongoing, capacity-building professional development is a top priority. We have *totally* embraced the belief that poverty is not an excuse for poor achievement.

- There is a strong commitment to excellence by the administration and the faculty. Our parent involvement is very good, and our parents help to make our school better.

- My teachers participate in professional development that allows them to provide input into instructional decisions. That means we have a very unified approach. My teachers are extremely dedicated.

- We have a very high-quality faculty and staff. We are a family! We have high-quality relationships with our parents. Good Teaching = Good Discipline. We really celebrate successes.

- Our staff is *dedicated*. They are open to new ideas because they want to help students learn. We *always* put student interests first.

We find these cornerstones of excellence both reassuring and unsettling—reassuring because every school could achieve them, unsettling because too few do.

Resources

Alexander, K. L., Entwisle, D. R., & Kabbani, N. S. (2001). The dropout process in life course perspective: Early risk factors at home and school. *Teacher College Record, 103*(5), 760–821.

Aloise-Young, P. A., & Chavez, E. L. (2002). Not all school dropouts are the same: Ethnic differences in the relation between reasons for leaving school and adolescent substance use. *Psychology in the Schools, 39*(5), 539–547.

Anderman, E. M., & Maehr, M. L. (1994). Motivation and schooling in the middle grades. *Review of Educational Research, 64*(2), 287–309.

Annie E. Casey Foundation (2003). *Kids count data book.* Baltimore: Author.

Barker, J. A. (1993). *Paradigms: The business of discovering the future.* New York: Harper Business.

Barr, R. D., & Parrett, W. H. (1997). *How to create alternative, magnet and charter schools that work.* Bloomington, IN: National Education Service.

Bernhardt, V. (1998). *Data analysis for continued school improvement.* Larchmont, NY: Eye On Education.

Blankstein, A. M. (2004). *Failure is not an option™: Six principles that guide student achievement in high-performing schools.* Thousand Oaks, CA: Corwin Press.

Bossidy, L, Charan, R. & Burk, C., (2002). *Execution: the discipline of getting things done.* Crown Publishers.

Bottoms, G. (2001). *Putting lessons learned to work: Improving the achievement of vocational students.* SREB Research Brief. Retrieved December 20, 2006, from http://www.sreb.org/programs/hstw/publications/briefs/lessons_learned.asp

Beaudoin, N., (2005). *Stepping outside your comfort zone: Lessons for school leaders.* Larchmont, NY: Eye On Education.

Beaudoin, N., (2005). *Elevating student voice: How to enhance participation, citizenship, and leadership.* Larchmont, NY: Eye On Education.

Blackburn, B., (2005). *Classroom motivation from A to Z: How to engage your students in learning.* Larchmont, NY: Eye On Education.

California Department of Alcohol and Drug Programs (1995). Drug use: Negative outcomes linked in dropout study. *Alcoholism and Drug Abuse Weekly, 7*(33), 2–4.

Carter, S. C. (2001). *No excuses: Lessons from 21 high-performing, high-poverty schools.* Washington, DC: The Heritage Foundation.

Castle, R. C. (1994). The dynamics of educational systems and low achieving dislocated students: An intellectual approach to school and business partnerships. In R.C. Morris (Ed.), *Using what we know about at-risk youth* (pp. 7–13). Lancaster, PA: Technomic Publishing Company.

Covey, S. (1990) *Principle-centered leadership.* NY: Summit Books.

Council of the Great City Schools (2003). *Urban school superintendents: Characteristics, tenure and salary. Fourth Biennial Survey.* Retrieved December 20, 2005, from http://www.cgcs.org/pdfs/2003IndicatorFinal.pdf

Croninger, R. G., & Lee, V. E. (2001). Social capital and dropping out of high school: Benefits to at-risk students of teacher support and guidance. *Teachers College Record, 103*(4), 548–581.

Davenport, P., & Anderson G. (2002). *Closing the achievement gap: No excuses.* Houston: American Productivity and Quality Center.

Dornbusch, S. M., Carlsmith, J. M., Bushwall, S. J., et al. (1985). Single parents, extended households, and the control of adolescents. *Child Development, 56,* 326–341.

Druian, G., & Butler, J. A., (2001). *Effective schooling practices and at-risk youth: What the research shows.* Portland, OR: Northwest Regional Education laboratory. Retrieved June 18, 2004, from http://www.nwrel.org/scpd/sirs/1/topsyn1.html

Duffy, F. (1996) Designing high-performance schools: A practical guide to organizational reengineering. Delray Beach, FL: St. Lucie.

Duttweiler, P. C. (1995). *Effective strategies for educating students in at-risk situations.* Clemson, SC: National Dropout Prevention Center.

Duttweiler, P. C., & Mutchler, S. E. (1991). *Organizing the educational system for excellence: Harnessing the energy of people.* Austin, TX: Southwest Educational Development Laboratory.

Dweyer, K., Osher, D., & Warger, C. (1998). *Early warning, timely response: A guide to safe schools.* Washington, DC: U.S. Department of Education.

Eccles, J. S., Early, D., Frasier, K., Belansky, E., & McCarthy, K. (1997). The relation of connection, regulation, and support for autonomy to adolescent functioning. *Journal of Adolescent Research, 12*(2), 263–286.

Eccles, J. S., Midgefield, C., & Wigfield, A. (1993). Development during adolescence: The impact of stage-environment fit on young adolescents' experiences in schools and in families. *American Psychologist, 48*(2), 90–101.

Engel, D. E. (1994). School leavers in American society: Interviews with school drop-outs/stop-outs. In R.C. Morris (Ed.), *Using what we know about at-risk youth* (pp.15–22). Lancaster, PA: Technomic Publishing Company.

Fiore, S., & Joseph, J. (2005). Making the right decisions: A guide for school leaders. Larchmont, NY: Eye On Education.

Friedman, T. (2005). The world is flat: A brief history of the twenty-first century. New York: Farrar, Straus & Giroux.

Gleason, P., & Dynarski, M. (2002). Do we know whom to serve? Issues in using risk factors to identify dropouts. *Journal of Education for Students at Risk, 7*(1), 25–41.

Gleaton, T. J. (2001, January). *Evaluating school safety and student drug use with PRIDE SURVEYS.* Bowling Green, KY: Author.

Gupton, S. L. (2002). *The instructional leadership toolbox: A handbook for improving practice.* Thousand Oaks, CA: Corwin Press.

Henry, T. (2000, June 26). Group to donate $150 million to develop school leaders. *USA Today,* p. D1.

Hodkinson, H. (2000). High school demographics demand change. *High School Magazine, 7*(May), 42–43.

Hoyt, K. B., & Van Dyke, L. A. (1958). *The Drop-out problem in Iowa high schools* (Report No. JXQ38625). Des Moines, IA: Iowa State Department of Public Instruction. (ERIC Document Reproduction Service No. ED002793)

Illich, I. (1970). *Deschooling society.* New York: Marion Boyers Publishers.

Jenkins, L. (1997) *Improving student learning, applying Deming's quality principles in classrooms.* Milwaukee, WI: Quality Press.

Jones, R. (1998). What works: Researchers tell what schools must do to improve student achievement. *American School Board Journal, 185*(April), 28–33.

Jordan, W. J., Lara, J., & McPartland, J. M. (1996). Exploring the causes of early dropout among race-ethnic and gender groups. *Youth and Society, 28*(1), 62–94.

Juran, J. (1989) *Juran on leadership for quality: An executive handbook.* New York: Free Press.

Kasen, S., & Cohen, P. (1998). Adolescent school experiences and dropout, adolescent pregnancy, and young adult deviant behavior. *Journal of Adolescent Research, 13*(1), 49–72.

Kominski, R., Jamieson, A., & Martinez, G. (2001). At-risk conditions of U.S. school-aged children (Working Paper Series No. 52). Washington, DC: U.S. Census Bureau.

Kortering, L. J., Konold, T. R., & Glutting, J. (1998). Comparing the reasons for coming to school among high school dropouts and nondropouts. *Journal of At-Risk Issues, 5*(1), 10–15.

Kozel, J. (2005) *The shame of the nation: The restoring of apartheid schooling in America.* New York: Crown Publishing Group.

Kubik, M. L., Lytle, L., & Fulkerson, J. A. (2004). Physical activity, dietary practices, and other health behaviors of at-risk youth attending alternative high schools. *Journal of School Health, 74*(4), 119–124.

Laffey, J. M., Espinosa, L., Moore, J., & Lodree, A. (2003). Supporting learning and behavior of at-risk young children: Computers in urban education. *Journal of Research on Technology in Education, 35*(4), 423–440.

Lagana, M. T. (2004). Protective factors for inner-city adolescents at risk of school dropout: Family factors and social support. *Children & Schools, 26*(4), 211–220.

Law, S. G., & Lane, D. S. (1987). Multicultural acceptance by teacher education students. *Journal of Instructional Psychology, 14*(1), 3–9.

Leithwood, K. A., & Riehl, C. (2003). *What we know about successful school leadership* (Brief of report prepared for the Taskforce on Developing Research in Educational Leadership, a division of the American Educational Research Association). Philadelphia PA: Laboratory for Student Success, Temple University.

Levine, A. (2005). *Educating school leaders.* Washington, DC: The Education Schools Project.

Lewis, T. J., & Sugai, G. (1999). Effective behavior support: A systems approach to proactive school-wide management. *Focus on Exceptional Children, 31*(6), 1–24.

Magdol, L. (1998). Risk factors for academic student achievement. In K. Bogenschneider & J. Olson (Eds.), *Enhancing educational performance: Three policy alternatives.* (Wisconsin Family Impact Seminar Briefing Report No. 11, pp. 1–14). Madison, WI: University of Wisconsin Center for Excellence in Family Studies.

Marzano, R. J., Pickering, D. J., & Pollock, J. E. (2001). *Classroom instruction that works: Research-based strategies for increasing student achievement.* Alexandria, VA: Association for Supervision and Curriculum Development.

McCluskey, C. P., Krohn, M. D., Lizotte, A. J., & Rodriguez, M. L. (2002). Early substance abuse and school achievement: An examination of Latino, white, and African-American youth. *Journal of Drug Issues, 32*(3), 921–943.

McNeely, C. A., Nonnemaker, J. M., & Blum, R. W. (2002). Promoting school connectedness: Evidence from the national longitudinal study of adolescent health. *Journal of School Health, 72*(4), 138–146.

Miller, C. A., Fitch, T., & Marshall, J. L., (2003). Locus of control and at-risk youth: A comparison of regular education high school students and students in alternative schools. *Education, 123*(3), 548–551.

Morris, R. C. (1994). *Using what we know about at-risk youth.* Lancaster, PA: Technomic Publishing.

National Center for Educational Statistics. (2001, November). *Statistical analysis report: Dropout rates in the United States: 2000.* Retrieved October 30, 2004, from http://nces.ed.gov/pubs2002/droppub_2001

National Center for Educational Statistics. (2002, August). *Public high school dropouts and completers from the common core of data: School years 1998–99 and 1999–2000.* Retrieved October 30, 2004, from http://nces.ed.gov/pubs2002/2002382.pdf

National Center for Educational Statistics. (2004, November). *Statistical analysis report: Dropout rates in the United States: 2001.* Retrieved July 8, 2005, from http://nces.ed.gov/pubs2005/2005046.pdf.

Natriello, G., & McDill, E. L. (1986). Performance standards, student effort on homework, and academic achievement. *Sociology of Education, 59*(1), 18–31.

Paine, L. (1989). *Orientation towards diversity: What do prospective teachers bring?* (Research Report 89–9). East Lansing, MI: National Center for Research on Teacher Learning.

Pascopella, A. (2003). Drop out. *District Administration, 38*(11), 32–36.

Pawlas, G. E. (2005). *The administrator's guide to school–community relations.* Larchmont, NY: Eye On Education.

Rothstein, R. (2004). *Class and schools: Using social, economic, and educational reform to close the black-white achievement gap.* New York: Teachers College Press.

Sapp, M., & Farrell, W. (1994). Cognitive-behavioral interventions: Applications for academically at-risk and special education students. *Preventing School Failure, 38*(2), 19–24.

Sarason, S. B. (1995). Some reactions to what we have learned. *Phi Delta Kappan, 77*(1), 84–85.

Schargel, F. P. (2005, March). *The George Westinghouse High School story.* Paper presented at the Alabama State University Dropout Prevention Center annual conference. Montgomery, AL.

Schargel, F. P., & Smink, J. (2001). *Strategies to help solve our school dropout problem.* Larchmont, NY: Eye On Education.

Schargel, F. P. (2001). *Dropout prevention tools.* Larchmont, NY: Eye On Education.

Schargel, F. P. (2005). *Best practices to help at-risk learners.* Larchmont, NY: Eye On Education.

Sexton, P. W. (1985). Trying to make it real compared to what: Implications of high school dropout statistics. *Journal of Educational Equity and Leadership, 5*(2), 92–106.

Shinn, K. (2002). Luring high school parents onto our turf. *The Education Digest, 67*(6), 34–36.

Smink, J., & Schargel F. P., (2004). *Helping students graduate: A strategic approach to dropout prevention.* Larchmont, NY: Eye On Education.

Somers, C. L., & Piliawsky, M. (2004). Drop-out prevention among urban, African American adolescents: Program evaluation and practical implications. *Preventing School Failure, 49*(3), 17–22.

Sprague, J., & Nishioka, V. (2004). Skills for success: A three-tiered approach to positive behavior supports. In V. Gaylord, D. R. Johnson, C. A. Lehr, C. D. Bremer, & S. Hasazi (Eds.), *Impact: Feature issue on achieving secondary and transition results for students with disabilities 16*(3), 16–18. Minneapolis: University of Minnesota, Institute of Community Integration. Retrieved June 18, 2004, from http://ici.umn.edu/products/impact/163/prof3.html

Steinberg, L. (1996). *Why school reform has failed and what parents need to do.* New York: Simon and Schuster.

Troy, F. J. (1998). The myth of our failed education system. *The School Administrator, 55*(9), 6–10.

Trubowitz, S. (1997). *How it works: Inside a school–college collaboration.* New York: Teachers College Press.

Tucker, M. (2002). *Building the capacity of schools, districts, and states to educate all students to high standards: The case of the America's choice school design.* Washington, DC: National Center on Education and the Economy.

U.S. Census Bureau (2004). *Families by age of householder, number of children, and family structure.* Retrieved March 10, 2005, from http://pubdb3.census.gov/macro/032004/pov/new04_100_06.htm

Vanderslice, R. (2004). Risky business: Leaving the at-risk child behind. *Delta Kappa Gamma Bulletin, 71*(1), 15–21.

Walsh, J., & Sattes, B., (2000) Inside school improvement: Creating a high-performing learning culture. Edvantia.

Wing-Lin, L. F., & Miu-Ling, I. F. (2003). Young school dropouts: Levels of influence of different systems. *Journal of Youth Studies, 6*(1), 89–110.

Zapeda, S. (2003) The principal as instructional leader: A handbook for supervisors. New York: Eye On Education.

Zapeda, S., & Mayers, R., (2004) Supervision across the content areas. New York: Eye On Education.